guidebook for speech communication

MILTON DICKENS
University of Southern California

JAMES H. McBATH
University of Southern California

HARCOURT BRACE JOVANOVICH, INC.
NEW YORK   CHICAGO   SAN FRANCISCO   ATLANTA

ISBN: 0-15-530006-7

Library of Congress Catalog Card Number: 73-2176

Printed in the United States of America

The four lines of poetry from "I Love You, California"
(*Look*, June 30, 1962) on page 108 are reprinted with
the permission of Richard Armour.

preface

This book is designed for use in the basic course in speech communication. Its aim is to assist students in gaining practical knowledge about the everyday requirements of spoken communication. While communication may be profitably read about and discussed, the improvement of individual communicative abilities requires a variety of guided, criticized experiences. The *Guidebook* is an instructional tool for converting sound theory into practice.

In deciding the assignments to be used in his course, the instructor may be assisted by considering the progression of projects presented in this guidebook, all of which have been tested by trial in the classroom. In his preplanning, the instructor may secure useful data at the first class meeting by having students complete and turn in the Personal Data Sheet and the inventory of Goals in This Course, pages vii and viii. If the instructor also wants an immediate assessment of the students' library-research knowledge, he may use the form on page 18.

Realizing that instructors differ in their teaching styles, we provide more projects than could possibly be covered in a single course; the instructor may select projects in accordance with his personal preferences. Likewise, flexibility is provided by presenting each project as an independent unit so as to facilitate rearrangements of assignment sequences.

Classroom time is conserved by using the book to share the job of making and explaining assignments. While the most essential and effective guidance is given orally by the instructor, either during class or in private conferences, there is a built-in time limit on the amount of such oral advice. Written critiques and the use of criticism charts save time and also provide students with a tangible record of their past progress and their immediate goals.

We believe that the book will usually be most effective when used in conjunction with a standard speech communication text. However, in special teaching situations, such as short courses and workshops, an instructor may prefer to use the *Guidebook* in conjunction with lectures and collateral readings. In either case, we hope that the book will help to systematize practice projects through which the students learn by doing.

This workbook is based on our earlier *Guidebook for Speech Practice.* It has been thoroughly revised and brought up to date to reflect recent research in communication theory. In addition, it has been influenced by feedback from many instructors who have used these projects in their beginning classes. Suggestions on specific projects were made by Julie McElhiney, LaDonna McMurray, and David Robinson, instructors in the basic speech program at the University of Southern California. Janet Bolton advised us on the Communicative Reading project. We gratefully acknowledge their contributions.

MILTON DICKENS
JAMES H. McBATH

contents

four

basic types of speech communication   105

five

special types of group and public communication   149

appendix   181
supplementary sections

personal data sheet

NAME _____ CLASS _____

CAMPUS ADDRESS _____ MAJOR _____

_____ TELEPHONE _____

HOME ADDRESS _____ MARRIED? _____

_____

OUTSIDE EMPLOYMENT _____

PROFESSIONAL GOAL _____

HIGH SCHOOL _____ YEAR OF GRADUATION _____

Present extracurricular activities:

Chief hobbies:

Previous speech training, if any:

Do you feel you have any specific problems in speech?

What are your anticipated uses of training received in this course?

goals in this course

NAME_____ CLASS_____

What do you most want to accomplish through this course?

Please rank your "top ten" goals in order of priority:

_____ to improve my voice and articulation

_____ to become more fluent

_____ to gain confidence and poise

_____ to deliver a speech effectively

_____ to learn about modern communication theories

_____ to work efficiently with small groups (e.g., committees)

_____ to organize my ideas more logically

_____ to become a better listener

_____ to improve my personality

_____ to influence audience behavior

_____ to become a better conversationalist

_____ to evaluate the speeches of others (e.g., political leaders)

_____ to analyze great speakers of the past

_____ to develop more efficient research methods

_____ to increase my speaking vocabulary

_____ to use nonverbal symbols (e.g., gestures) more effectively

_____ to test some of my ideas by getting reactions from the class

_____ other (write in your own goal if it does not appear above)

one

conversational speech communication

You learned to talk as a child; you have been talking ever since. With most of us, the development of speaking and listening habits was a remarkably haphazard process: we learned from our parents, from other relatives, playmates, school teachers—from practically anybody; we were influenced by movies and TV and radio; we were influenced by reading everything from comic books to classics. So it should come as no surprise to learn that some of your speaking and listening habits are poor ones, some are good, and others in-between. And it is likely that you cannot tell which is which—because you are so used to them all. During this term you will want to take regular inventories of your oral communication attitudes and habits. You will want to retain and capitalize on the effective ones, improve the indifferent ones, unlearn and replace the undesirable ones. You will accomplish your goals largely by means of *practice with guidance.* Guidance will be provided by your textbook, your instructor, and your fellow students.

We will begin with some projects involving informal conversational communication. This is the kind of talking that you do most often. Furthermore, it is fundamentally the same process as the speech communication you do in less familiar, more formal situations. Thus, this guidebook provides practice projects that not only embody the educational philosophy of learning by doing, but also provide for applying the unifying principle of progressing by gradual and natural steps from the relatively simple through the more complex speaking situations.

class discussion:
"the study of speech communication"

OBJECTIVE

Some students enter a speech communication class fearfully, expecting an ordeal when facing an audience; others enter nonchalantly, expecting an easy course because speech is a familiar personal activity. Neither attitude is justified. And there are other popular misconceptions about speech work. As a consequence it is wise to begin your study of speech with a review of your beliefs and attitudes on the subject. A class discussion should indicate which attitudes to avoid and which to develop as you approach the study of oral communication.

BACKGROUND

You have had years of experience with class discussions—dating back probably to kindergarten days—yet you may never have paused to analyze and evaluate this experience. A speech class is a good place to practice to become a better participant in any classroom discussion. You will increase the effectiveness of your classwork, not only in speech communication but also in every other course that you take. What do most instructors expect of you?

you are expected to participate

Some students prefer merely to sit back and listen. If everyone indulged that preference, the class discussion would consist of—silence.

Contribute facts. You are expected not only to say something, but also to have something to say. Almost every class discussion focuses upon previously assigned readings or activities. If you have done the required preparation, you will have worthwhile information to contribute at appropriate times during the class discussion.

Express your opinions. One difference between formal recitation and informal discussion is that the latter encourages not only the presentation of facts but also the expression of personal opinions based upon independent thinking about the facts. Usually that thinking should have been done before the meeting. Occasionally, however, a judgment formed on the spur of the moment, whether sound or faulty, may help to spark the discussion. Personal opinions should be offered constructively.

Ask questions. You may direct a question to the instructor when you are genuinely in doubt about particular ideas being discussed or about the discussion procedures. You may question another student to secure clarification of statements he has just made, or to suggest weaknesses in his position. You may direct a question to the class as a whole in order to call attention to important points that have been overlooked, or to invite a variety of viewpoints, or to rekindle the discussion if it is dying down.

you are expected to control your participation

Be relevant. Follow the discussion alertly at all times, and when you join in, speak to the point and stick to the point. Only rarely should you leap backward ("If you don't mind, I'd like to go back to a point that came up a few minutes ago") or leap ahead before the immediate point has been concluded. ("This is all very interesting but I think we have entirely missed the really important question.")

Be brief. Classroom time is limited, the ideas to be discussed are many, and all the members of the class have a right to be heard. So make your remarks as brief as is consistent with clarity. If you have nothing to contribute, do not waste the time of others who are better prepared—your instructor and many of the students have long since learned to detect bluffing.

Be courteous. Taking an active part in discussion does not mean elbowing others out of your way. After you have spoken a few times, look the class over and mentally check those who have not yet been heard. If any of them want to participate, give them a chance. If a few overaggressive or overtalkative students are crowding out their more polite or more reticent colleagues, help the latter group. ("I'd like to hear from some of the class who haven't yet had a chance to discuss this point.")

INSTRUCTIONS

Preparation for this class discussion of "The Study of Speech Communication" should include the following activities:

1. Take the Attitudes Test on page 5. Give your honest opinion regarding each item. The test will be scored and discussed in class.
2. Read at least one popularized article or chapter on speech from a newspaper, nontechnical magazine, or nonacademic book. Take notes regarding the author's attitudes and assumptions concerning the learning of better speech.

3. Informally interview five or six people to discover some of their attitudes and assumptions toward speech, keeping appropriate notes. Try to think of questions which will indirectly draw out clues to their basic beliefs. Some sample questions: Who do you think is the best political speaker in the United States today, and why do you think so? Does the study of written composition and grammar provide sufficient training for the use of the spoken word? What is the main difference between conversation and public speaking?

NAME _____ DATE _____

Below is an attitudes test. Please mark each item by circling the "T" or the "F." Simply indicate your present opinion as to whether a given statement is true or false. Your score will have no bearing upon your grade in this course.

T F   1. The study of speech communication dates back to ancient times.

T F   2. The most important test of speaking effectiveness is *always* in terms of audience response.

T F   3. By and large public speakers are born, not made.

T F   4. The aim of a speaking course is to teach the student to speak at any time, on any subject, with a minimum of preparation.

T F   5. There are several fundamental differences between public speaking and conversation.

T F   6. *How* you say a thing is more important than *what* you say.

T F   7. There are five vowel sounds in the English language (and sometimes two more).

T F   8. Most of our greatest speakers and actors still experience a great deal of stage fright.

T F   9. There is only one absolutely correct pronunciation for any given word.

T F   10. "Gestures" should be defined as movements of the arms and hands.

T F   11. An extemporaneous talk is one given without preparation.

T F   12. A good speaker should never lean on the rostrum or other furniture.

T F   13. In reading poetry aloud, the reader should pause at each comma, period, or end of a line.

T F   14. The first step in the efficient preparation of a public speech is to write a manuscript or at least an outline.

T F   15. The proper way to close any given speech is to say, "I thank you."

CLASS DISCUSSION: "THE STUDY OF SPEECH COMMUNICATION"

2

knowing the class

OBJECTIVE

This opening project has a dual purpose: to enable class members to know their immediate audience, and to collect information about the group that will be useful in preparation for later projects.

BACKGROUND

Everyone during his lifetime speaks to a variety of audiences, ranging from one to many other persons. Each auditor brings to the listening situation his attitudes, ideas, associations, and stored-up experiences; he will tend to interpret what he hears in the light of his own life history. So the audience is central to speech communication. Knowing the interests and attitudes of these listeners can help in shaping your answers to such speech-building factors as topic selection, formulation of speech purposes, laying out major lines of development, selecting supporting materials, and even choice of language. Your audience plays the key role in these decisions.

During the present term you will speak a number of times to this class, whose members are your audience. You can learn some important things about them by direct observation (including age and sex). What else about this audience do you need to know that would help you to make sensible choices in reaching them? How can you go about learning what you wish to know? The point of this project can be stated simply: "Let's ask them." Fortunately, in the class we have an opportunity to poll members about themselves and to discuss their responses. In order to gain our information systematically, an informal survey can be made by a class-constructed questionnaire. Here are a few suggestions about designing your questionnaire:

1. Decide on questions the answers to which will evoke useful information about common traits and interests (for example, political preferences, majors, occupational goals, attitudes toward campus or public issues, and so on). Avoid redundant or irrelevant questions and those with obvious answers.
2. Be sure to provide a clear set of instructions for answering. These guidelines are particularly important if the questionnaire is to be self-administered.
3. Phrase questions carefully to reduce the chances that any of them will be misunderstood. Each question should be concerned with one topic only.
4. Construct the questionnaire so it can be tabulated efficiently. Often the *closed form* of questionnaire (where the respondent circles or checks one of several alternate answers) is superior to the *open form* (where the respondent must formulate his own reply).
5. Structure the questionnaire so that items are arranged in a common-sense order, usually with easy-to-answer questions coming first.
6. Pretest questions to see if they produce the kinds of responses that are useful. Some questions that seem perfectly reasonable to you may lead or mislead respondents.
7. Be sure that the questionnaire adequately protects the anonymity of the respondents.

(These suggestions will ordinarily suffice for the informal class poll. Later, if the class wishes to consider survey techniques in detail, references such as the following will be helpful: Backstrom and Hursh, *Survey Research* (1963); Hyman, *Survey Design and Analysis* (1955); Oppenheim, *Questionnaire Design and Attitude Measurement* (1966).

INSTRUCTIONS

1. Divide the class into groups of about six to eight members. Each group will develop a questionnaire designed to secure the information you would like to have about members of this class. What would you most like to know about this audience?

2. Upon recommendation of the instructor, choose a plan for development and administration (for example, the several questionnaires might be administered separately, or the class might decide on the best combination of items to be incorporated into a single questionnaire).

3. The questionnaires are duplicated, completed by class members, and the results are tallied.

4. The instructor may lead a discussion of the results and their implications at the next class period. Topics such as these often come up in discussions about the audience as a communication variable: Is there a difference between an audience and a group of individual auditors? What statements can be made about listeners simply by looking at them? If it is impossible to administer a questionnaire (as the class has just done), how can the speaker learn what he wants to know about his audience? Does a speaker pander to an audience by adapting his speech to them? What ethical considerations are raised in a speaker's adjusting his message to the attitudes and beliefs of his listeners? If a speaker discovers that all his listeners already agree with him, what functions does his speech then serve?

3

interviews

OBJECTIVE

The previous project helped you to know the class as a group. This project focuses on individual members of the class; it enables you to know them better as people. A secondary aim is to introduce you to the interview as an instrument for getting and giving information.

BACKGROUND

Conversations in which one person requests information and another supplies it are common in all human experience. We carry on such dialogues almost continuously with friends, family, teachers, employers, and casual acquaintances. From this stream of shared messages we know increasingly well how various people feel, what they think, what they may do or attempt, how they characteristically approach problems, and the like. The more frequent and intense our interaction with a person, the more fully informed we are likely to be about him and the more accurate we become in predicting and understanding his behavior.

The interview is defined as an informal, yet structured, pattern of communicative interaction between two persons, initiated for a specific purpose and focused on some particular content area. Put simply: it is a planned discussion between two people on a subject that they both want or need to explore. As in any communication event, messages are constantly being sent and received by the participants. These messages may be verbal or nonverbal, intentional or unintentional. W. Charles Redding has described interviewing as "probably the most fundamental and most frequently occurring form of human communication."

preparation check list

Because the purpose of this project is one of informal information and attitude sharing among class members, several suggestions can serve as a useful preparation check list:

1. Decide first on the specific purposes of your interview. Devise a set of questions keyed to the major types of information sought. Do not prepare a list of questions to be read mechanically in an inflexible sequence to the interviewee.
2. The atmosphere should be conducive to a free and friendly exchange. Establish a good relationship at the outset.
3. If you think a respondent has more to tell, pursue the point: "Anything else?" "Will you explain?" "Yes, but why?"
4. Maintain a receptive attitude toward responses. This is not the time to quibble or argue, even if you disagree with the view expressed.
5. Sometimes it is helpful to rephrase questions and to summarize periodically to be sure you understand each other.

6. Use simple, familiar language.
7. Try not to intrude yourself into the interview session. Use as few words as necessary. Your object is to learn about the *other* person.
8. Be alert for nonverbal cues. The respondent's emphasis, tone of voice, physical behavior, facial expression, and so on, may provide insights into his reactions to the questions.
9. Use a system of note-taking that is adequate to your purposes, yet is unobtrusive. Listening and observing are your most important tasks.

(For those who wish to pursue their interest in interviewing, sources such as these can be consulted: Bingham, Moore, and Gustad, *How to Interview* (1969); Black, *How to Get Results from Interviewing* (1970); Goyer, Redding, and Rickey, *Interviewing Principles and Techniques* (1968); Kahn and Cannell, *The Dynamics of Interviewing* (1957).

INSTRUCTIONS

1. The class will be divided into "interview groups" of four or five members each. So that each member will know the others in his assigned group and how to reach them, names and telephone numbers of group members should be recorded and distributed:

Members of Group

A. _____
B. _____
C. _____
D. _____
E. _____

Interviews outside of class. The first round of interviews will take place outside of class. Each person will engage in two out-of-class interviews; he will interview one person, and he will be interviewed by one other person. The person interviewing should attempt to learn as much as possible about the person he interviews.

4-Way Interview Group

A interviews B
B interviews C
C interviews D
D interviews A

5-Way Interview Group

A interviews B
B interviews C
C interviews D
D interviews E
E interviews A

Interviews in class. The second round of interviews will take place in class. In each case the original interviewer is himself interviewed about his subject (for example, A interviews C about D). Each interview session will run about 15 minutes. Approximately 10 minutes will be devoted to the interview, during which time the other class members should *not* interrupt. In the remaining 5 minutes the class may offer comments or questions, reserving a final brief opportunity for rejoinder from the "victim."

4-Way Interview Group

A interviews C about D
B interviews D about A
C interviews A about B
D interviews B about C

5-Way Interview Group

A interviews C about D
B interviews D about E
C interviews E about A
D interviews A about B
E interviews B about C

The assignment may be concluded by one of the following options:

Class discussion. At the end of the last interview (on the second day of interviews), the class may discuss generalizations that can be made about the interviewing process.

Written report. Each class member will make a written report on what he has learned about the process of interviewing. Reference should be made to the nine suggestions in the preparation check list.

2. The second assignment simulates an employment interview. The class is paired into teams of two, with one member serving as interviewer and the other as interviewee. The interviewee (applicant) prepares a one-paragraph description of the position sought and a one-page résumé that presents the applicant's qualifications and essential personal information: name, address, phone number, and such data as career objectives, education, work experience, military service and status, personal background and interests, and references. If class members (or a panel of critics) receive copies of the *job description* and *résumé*, they are prepared to comment on the skill of the interviewer in eliciting essential information and the effectiveness of the interviewee in presenting himself as an acceptable candidate. As background for the project, it is useful to invite an industrial placement representative or a school placement officer to describe his typical interview experiences.

A variation of the job interview assignment calls for two or more teams of three to five members each. One member is designated as the interviewer (employer); two or more other members are interviewees (applicants). Each group agrees to a one-paragraph written job description. Thus, two or more applicants are competing for the same job. At the conclusion, the interviewer and all other members of the class (observers) cast ballots indicating which one of the competing applicants should be chosen. If time permits, a class discussion is held to evaluate the skills of each interviewer and each interviewee.

brainstorming

OBJECTIVE

To experience an informal problem-solving process that is efficient in producing new ideas and to learn more about members of the class by providing a situation that encourages involvement and interaction.

BACKGROUND

Brainstorming is a relatively unstructured, accelerated process of group discussion. Originated by Alex F. Osborn, an advertising executive, the technique is especially useful when the marshaling of the whole group's creative resources is required in a limited time. Besides providing a profusion of fresh ideas, the free-wheeling procedure tends to stimulate innovative contributions that might be inhibited by more formal discussion formats. Complex problems requiring study and analysis obviously call for problem-solving methods. But for concrete familiar subjects, brainstorming is a practical procedure for unlocking the stored-up thoughts of the group. Thus topics like "What should be our policy toward Africa?" or "What should be the role of students in university governance?" aren't suitable for brainstorming. But topics like "Ways to increase tourism to our state" or "Suggestions for improving the image of this school" could be profitably brainstormed.

To promote the openness, involvement, and constructive atmosphere of brainstorming, several ground rules should be agreed upon:

1. **Critical judgment is ruled out.** Evaluation of ideas must be withheld for later consideration. Good ideas often are stifled in their infancy by being considered farfetched; yet if permitted to mature, the same ideas would prove reasonable and defensible.

2. **Originality is encouraged.** Going beyond the conventional and the obvious is imperative. The more novel the suggestion, the better; it is easier to modify ideas and plans than to construct them from scratch. Even the offbeat and impractical may suggest workable alternatives.

3. **Productivity is essential.** The greater the quantity, the greater the likelihood of winners. No limit is placed on the number of contributions any member can make. Freed from censorship, a good brain-storming period may produce 50 to 75 suggestions that might be generalized into 10 or 15 useful recommendations.

4. **Combination and improvement are prized.** In addition to contributing ideas of their own, participants should suggest how ideas of others can be turned into better ideas; or how two or more suggestions can be combined into still another idea. It is perfectly acceptable to "hitchhike" on someone else's suggestion.

Several specific recommendations are useful in arranging the brainstorming session:

1. The ideal group size is about 8 to 10 members (but the group can be much larger).

2. The problem should be specific, clear, and immediate.

3. The suggested time limit of 20 minutes per topic can be shortened or extended, depending on the pace of contributions.

4. So that members are free to think and contribute, a full-time reporter should be appointed to take down ideas. Use a tape recorder if the group is small and room acoustics are good.

5. The leader must exert a positive influence; he should prevent premature criticism or negative reaction to contributions. Contributions should be brief, rapid-fire, and without elaboration or discussion.

6. Use mixed groups if possible—those with experience and those new to the problem, men and women, blacks and whites, and so on. A variety of contributions will tend to stimulate greater variety in responses.

7. Stimulate attitudes of mutual encouragement. A consultant to General Electric observed: "Form the habit of reacting *yes* to a new idea. First, think of all the reasons why it's good; there will be plenty of people around to tell you why it won't work."

INSTRUCTIONS

1. Choose a fairly specific topic, one that is within the interest and expertise of class members (for example, proposals relating to a well-known campus or community problem).

2. Select a moderator whose aim will be to encourage profuse suggestions and to promote a climate of openness and acceptance.

3. Name a secretary whose responsibility is the recording of all ideas in their order of presentation (even including suggestions that seemingly are repetitious or irrelevant). Someone may also be appointed to tape-record the session.

4. After the brainstorming session, the moderator and the secretary can consolidate similar suggestions and organize the list into major clusters. Results are reported to the class for further modification and consensus.

5. Alternatively, all suggestions can be written on a chalkboard, with the class participating in consolidation and revision.

5

active role of the listener

OBJECTIVE

This project provides a supplementary exercise that may be appropriately added to almost any subsequent speaking project. It requires that all students listen thoughtfully to one another during classroom activi-ties, and it guides that listening by providing a specific listening goal—responding almost immediately to a speaker's ideas by giving a brief impromptu commentary.

BACKGROUND

In an ordinary conversation with a friend, the two of you talk in alternation but both of you are listening simultaneously all of the time. As you hear yourself talking, you may show it by occasionally correcting errors or by making other changes as you go along. Meanwhile, you do not listen to your friend passively like a tape recorder—you talk back to him internally as he speaks, perhaps preplanning your next remarks. If he were saying the same things on television and you were listening with one or two companions, these covert responses might become overt—TV listeners often make remarks aloud to one another as they listen together to the speaker on the screen.

To return to the tape recorder analogy, if you talk for a minute or two to your friend, you cannot "rewind" him and "play back" your exact words. If in-stead you ask him to repeat or summarize your last statements, you will receive his interpretation of them, usually with some additional responses indicating his agreement, disagreement, or other evaluations.

Surveys have shown that you spend substantially more time in listening than in talking, reading, and writing combined. Furthermore, your effectiveness as a communicator depends in large measure upon how well you listen and how well you adjust to your own listeners. A good listener is not expected to memorize every word he hears, but he should learn to grasp the main ideas accurately. Still more important, the good listener should learn to make sensitive evaluations and to respond creatively. The act of listening is in and of itself an active response; the major question becomes how good it is.

INSTRUCTIONS

To assist you in becoming a better listener, your instructor may make a continuing assignment for selected projects during the remainder of this course. On days when several class members are scheduled to give prepared talks, everyone else will listen with a view to giving a brief response to one of the speakers. One way of handling the assignment is as follows.

At the conclusion of all of the prepared speeches the instructor allots a period of time for responses. The instructor chooses at random from the audience, first one student and then another who rises and gives his impromptu remarks directed to any of the speeches he has just heard. Thus, when you are among the listeners you will not know on what days or at what moment you may be called on. But each day you must be ready. This means that you must listen to your classmates attentively and purposively; often you will want to take some notes. When you give a response, you may either agree or disagree with the speaker; you may want to strengthen one of his points or to criticize his facts or logic. In any case, try to be constructive, and at least let the speaker know of some of your thoughts which ordinarily would have remained internal and unsaid.

Thus during the rest of the term you should get at least one and probably several chances to "talk back" to fellow students whose speeches have aroused your admiration or, sometimes, exasperation. Also, when you are one of the prepared speakers, you will get some overt feedback revealing the kinds of reactions that run through your listeners' minds and thus suggesting ways for you to become a more effective speech communicator.

two

organizing and developing ideas

About sixty years ago, John B. Watson, the father of behaviorism, proposed the intriguing theory that silent thinking is essentially talking to oneself. Other theorists have argued that language and thought are closely related but not identical. The controversy is still unresolved, and it is still being pursued by researchers in psychology, neurophysiology, linguistics, and communication. In either case we are confronted by the chicken-and-egg dilemma: to improve our mastery of language, we must improve our thinking, but vice versa, to improve our thinking we must improve our mastery of language!

The beginning student may well have reached by now the common-sense conclusion that the study of speech communication includes more than he had previously supposed. He is not here to learn the art of saying nothing well. He is here to improve his mastery of spoken language symbols which are simultaneously the chief vehicles or tools of his own thinking and of his efforts to intermingle his thinking with that of other people. What he learns pays double dividends.

Hence, beginning with this section we will focus upon the handling of verbal symbolizations, usually called "ideas." You will practice to improve your abilities to gather data, reason from them logically, and transmit the resultant ideas effectively to your listening audience.

6

gathering speech materials

OBJECTIVE

Worthwhile ideas must be derived from a knowledge of subject matter, that is, relevant data. This section deals with the collecting and recording of data. It provides a useful list of sources of speech materials and suggests some practical research practices.

BACKGROUND

In gathering materials for speechmaking there are at least three major sources:
1. Observation (informal or planned)
2. Conversation (including interviews)
3. Reading (including use of a library)
You have often noticed that speeches are enlivened by stories of personal experiences, quotations from personal correspondence, or reports of firsthand interviews. Usually, however, the speaker's ideas should also be supported by references, quotations, or summaries from authoritative written materials. You will sound egotistical if you constantly sprinkle your talk with "I believe," "I think," or "in my estimation." Your ideas may rightly be viewed with suspicion if you omit specific references in favor of such phrases as "statistics show," "experts have found," and "authorities agree." Your treatment of a subject will be superficial if you restrict your reading to one source, such as a magazine article or a chapter from a book. You should always know a great deal more about your topic than you could possibly squeeze into the time limits of your speech.

Students sometimes suppose that library research consists of consulting the card catalogue and finding a few textbooks and classics. But you have dozens of other sources—pamphlets, ads, news reports, paperbacks, almanacs, or even comic books can sometimes provide the needed facts, examples, or opinions. Every good library contains files of old periodicals and newspapers, hundreds of pamphlets, and sometimes filmstrips and phonograph records. Ask your librarian for indexes to such materials and practice using these indexes, especially such common ones as the *Readers'* *Guide to Periodical Literature* and the *New York Times Index.*

You should also know about the hundreds of convenient general reference books and the specialized guides to research. A check list of some common ones is provided on pages 18–19.

You may think that you already know everything necessary for adequate library research. To test this possibility, turn immediately to page 18 and fill in the Information Inventory; your instructor may wish to have you turn in the results.

Form the habit of recording the results of your research promptly, accurately, and systematically; use a notebook, scrapbook, vertical file folders, or a card file box. In recording and filing materials, consider the following suggestions:

1. Give each item a caption or "headline" by which you can quickly find it when needed.
2. Be certain that documentation is complete: author, title, date, and page.
3. If you quote directly from a reading, be sure to enclose the material in quotation marks. If portions of direct quotations are omitted, indicate omissions by dots (known as ellipses); respect the author's meaning.
4. If the discussion of a point is lengthy or the facts or statistics are numerous, you may summarize in your own words. If so, do not use quotation marks. Respect the author's meaning.
5. If possible, save the original source or a photocopy. Newspaper clippings, excerpts from magazines, and pamphlets often can be filed in original form. *But never clip anything from library copies.*

INSTRUCTIONS

Begin the collection of materials on a speech topic which you plan to discuss later in this course. Bring to class ten pieces of information on your topic, one card each from the following sources: a book, a periodical, a newspaper, a pamphlet, an encyclopedia, a book of quotations, an almanac, an atlas, *Who's Who,* and either *Statesman's Yearbook* or *Statistical Abstract of the United States.* Do not use secondary sources; prepare each card with primary document "in hand."

Record your information as follows:
1. Use four-by-six-inch file cards.
2. Record only one idea per card.
3. On the top line write a caption or headline in capital letters.
4. On the second line write the source; make it complete.
5. Skip a line and then write your notes, or paste a clipping or a photocopy. Use the back of the card if necessary.

INFORMATION INVENTORY

1. What books would you consult for brief quotations, topically listed? _____
_____

2. What references can you consult for information about people deceased during the last several years (e.g., FBI's J. Edgar Hoover)? _____
_____

3. Where would you find a brief chronological summary of the major news events of the past year?
_____

4. Can you name two or three periodicals that deal with the field of education? _____

5. What is the best guide to current and past New York City (and national) daily news? _____
_____

6. Where would you find regularly updated authoritative accounts of significant scientific theories, researches, and inventions? _____
_____

7. What special information is contained in each of the following?
   a. *Congressional Digest* _____
   b. *Congressional Record* _____
   c. *Roget's Thesaurus* _____
   d. *Keesing's Contemporary Archives* _____
   e. *Facts on File* _____
   _____

8. Do you need a research assignment?   yes   no

CHECK LIST OF REFERENCE BOOKS

For brief quotations (classified and conveniently indexed):
  Dictionary of Quotations, Evans
  Familiar Quotations, Bertlett
  Home Book of Quotations, Stevenson
  New Cyclopedia of Practical Quotations, Hoyt
  Oxford Dictionary of Quotations
Speech students should be familiar with three dictionaries:
  Funk & Wagnalls, New Standard Dictionary
  Random House Dictionary of the English Language
  Webster's Third New International Dictionary
And two other wordbooks:
  Roget's International Thesaurus
  Webster's Dictionary of Synonyms
For handy reference to facts and statistics of almost every kind:
  Information Please Almanac
  New York Times Encyclopedic Almanac
  Statistical Abstract of the United States
  Statesman's Yearbook
  World Almanac and Book of Facts
For information about national and world events:
  Congressional Quarterly Weekly Report
  Facts on File
  Keesing's Contemporary Archives
For information about people:
  Current Biography
  Dictionary of American Biography
  Webster's Biographical Dictionary
  Who's Who in America
  Many other specialized *Who's Who* volumes
For historical facts:
  Concise Dictionary of American History
  Dictionary of Dates and Anniversaries, Collison
  Encyclopedia of American Facts and Dates, Carruth
  Encyclopedia of World History, Langer
For geographical facts:
  Columbia Lippincott Gazetteer of the World
  Webster's Geographical Dictionary
Reports of speeches in Congress, plus miscellaneous material:
  Congressional Record
For summaries of current controversial questions:
  Congressional Digest
  Reference Shelf series
For general factual materials:
  Collier's Encyclopedia
  Encyclopedia Americana
  Encyclopaedia Britannica
  World Book Encyclopedia
For oddities:
  Famous First Facts, Kane
  Guinness Book of World Records
  Things Not Generally Known, Wells
  What Happened When, Mirkin

7

the speech unit: deductive

OBJECTIVE

The purpose of this project is to provide practice in (1) the statement of an abstract idea epitomized in one carefully worded sentence, and (2) the clarification of that statement by effective use of selected types of supportive details. This experience will introduce you to the key concept called the *speech unit,* which is a natural starting point for the study of how to organize and to outline speech materials.

BACKGROUND

The deceptively simple statement "I am against censorship" can have different meanings for different people. In a serious discussion, the statement could not stand by itself—it would have to be supported (or developed) by some contextual materials, probably including some specifics. However, if you were to plunge immediately into arguments supporting your position, you would unnecessarily risk misunderstandings. Probably you should say something like, "Let me tell you exactly what I mean and what I do not mean by the term 'censorship.' " This transitional sentence leads into materials aimed at supporting your statement by clarifying it; this particular transition also promises two subpoints (the *do's* and *do not's*). You now have available several appropriate forms of support: restatement (using different words), explanation (including definitions), description (of concrete objects or events), and quotations (probably from authorities on your topic). In perspective, this hypothetical example illustrates a deductive sequence (from general to specific).

Broadening our discussion from the above particular example so as to include speech construction in general, we note the three fundamental tasks: stating a point, supporting it, and making transitions. Taken together, they form what we shall call a *speech unit.* We now have four concepts which are operationally defined as follows:

1. A speech unit comprises a speech point, its supports, and the needed transitions.
2. A speech point is the statement of a single idea in one declarative sentence.
3. A support is a clarification, reinforcement, or proof of a point.
4. A transition is a statement which leads the listener from one idea to the next by showing the relationship between the two ideas.

Later on, we will discuss these definitions and concepts in greater detail. Just now, however, it will suffice to become thoroughly familiar with the terms and to try them out in a brief speaking assignment.

The assignment focuses on an important problem in your everyday social relations—clarifying the verbal symbolization of abstract ideas. Such symbols are inherently ambiguous; this makes them one of the most common causes of "communication breakdowns."

INSTRUCTIONS

Choose a topic and derive from it the careful statement of your main point. Notice the difference between stating a topic and stating a speech point. If you say, "This morning I'm going to talk about the art of being natural," that is not a point—it is the announcement of a topic or general subject. Furthermore, "the art of being natural" is an abstraction with various possible meanings. Ask yourself such questions as: "What *about* it? What questions and expectations would the phrase arouse in my listeners' minds?" A variety of potential main points, some of them contradictory, will emerge: "The art of being natural means seeking truth through sensory experience." "Naturalism is itself unnatural." "The urge to return to nature is an instinctive human need." "The cult of returning to nature is a retreat from reality." Choose the point that expresses your view clearly and succinctly.

Having stated your main point, turn to planning how to clarify the abstract term. The necessity for doing this, in the example above, is demonstrated by psychologist Daniel Yankelovich in an article on student attitudes in the *Saturday Review*: "We have identified almost twenty meanings of the concept 'natural' as the student movement defines it." In developing your own meaning of the term, use two or more of these forms of support: restatement, explanation, description, and quotation. For instance, you might restate: "I mean the right to live as a human being, and not as a Social Security number or an electronic robot." Likewise, spell out your meaning by explaining concretely, by offering an operational definition, or by quoting someone who phrases your thought better than you can. (Other common forms of support, but *not* to be used in this project, are anecdotes, instances, statistics, and visual aids—they will be discussed later.)

Organize your talk deductively in accordance with the following sequence:

1. **Opening.** State the main point of the talk.
2. **Transition.** Get from the statement of your point into the supporting materials.
3. **Development.** Your main task is to clarify your point. In using each form of support try to keep it brief, simple, concrete, interesting.
4. **Transition.** Get from the supporting materials into your concluding statements.
5. **Conclusion.** Summarize or restate your point.

Your delivery of this talk should be concerned with only two things:

1. **Directness.** Talk with your classmates. Look at them. Think in terms of their reactions. Be friendly and communicative.
2. **Animation.** Show by facial expression, mood, and manner that you are alert, interested, enthusiastic.

Practice your talk aloud several times before coming to class. When you give the talk, you may use notes, but do not rely upon them too heavily. A few key words or phrases on a three-by-five-inch card should suffice. Study the Criticism Chart, pages 23–24.

SUGGESTED TOPICS

Political left-wingers	Academic freedom
Existentialism	Ethics of . . .
Systems engineering	The nature of prayer
DNA and heredity	Our tax system
The sexual revolution	Investment principles
Laissez faire	Due process of law
Bigotry	"The public interest,
Desegregation	convenience,
Environmental pollution	and necessity"
The laser principle	Drug addiction
Cybernetics	Theory of . . .

NAME_____ TIME _____ TO _____ TOTAL _____

TOPIC_____

Opening 1 2 3 4 5*

    Main point: stated—not stated; clear—not clear enough; too brief—wordy, abstract, technical, involved

Transition 1 2 3 4 5

    Adequate—fair—lacking; brief, smooth, appropriate—wordy, awkward, inappropriate

Development of point 1 2 3 4 5

    Forms of support used: Restatement? Explanation? Description? Quotation?
    How effective: brief, simple, clear, adequate—wordy, complicated, hard to understand, inadequate; concrete, specific—abstract, vague; interesting—dull; compact—rambling

    Other comments:

Conclusion 1 2 3 4 5

    Summary or restatement: adequate—fair—lacking; appropriate—inappropriate; smooth—too abrupt

    Directness: excellent, partial, lacking; looked at audience—looked at floor, ceiling, walls, out of window, over the heads, at notes, at one person or part of audience—eyes shifty, faraway look; general manner aloof, condescending, reserved, passive, impersonal, uncertain—friendly, poised, communicative, forceful, intense

*On the rating scale, 1 means far below average; 2, somewhat below average; 3, average; 4, somewhat above average; 5, superior.

Animation: facial expression excellent—partial—lacking—overdone—inappropriate; general
  manner lively, enthusiastic, alert—listless, colorless, stolid

Other comments:

the speech unit: inductive

OBJECTIVE

This project provides another way of practicing a *speech unit* (points, supports, transitions); in contrast to the preceding assignment, you will reverse the organizational sequence and you will utilize a different form of support. This time the sequence will be induc-

tive (from specific to general) and the form of support will be the anecdote. Structurally, your talk will resemble one of Aesop's fables—the narrating of a story with the "moral" stated at the end.

BACKGROUND

An inductive sequence has at least two special values for the communicator: (1) catching the listener's attention by arousing curiosity and creating suspense; (2) avoiding the danger of immediate rejection of the main point by delaying the statement of the point until after some acceptable supportive detail has favorably predisposed the listener's mind. The anecdote is an especially appropriate way of undertaking either of the foregoing tasks.

Anecdotes are probably the most widely used means of supporting points in speeches. They offer the speaker a potent technique for clarifying and reinforcing his thoughts. They may be true or hypothetical, serious or humorous, literal or figurative, or combinations of these; they may be straight narration or take the form of an analogy, a parable, or a fable. The best speech anecdote has these characteristics:

1. It must fit the speech. It is not dragged in for its own sake.

2. It has human interest. It arouses curiosity and concern over the outcome.
3. It is comparatively brief. Attention wanders during a narrative of tiresome length.
4. Its point is clear. Repetition or explanation diminishes its effectiveness.
5. Its details are specific. Names, places, and dates add to its interest.
6. It is in good taste. If you are in doubt, don't use it. *Unfavorable* attention is counterproductive.
7. It must be well told. Practice before you tell it to an audience.

A clever story often is remembered after other details of a speech are forgotten. If the anecdote is well chosen and skillfully presented, it will stick in listeners' minds as a reminder of the main point you were discussing.

INSTRUCTIONS

Collect good anecdotes and file them for later use. Select appropriate ones for your next speech; use one or two in almost any speech. Practice relating anecdotes in a direct, animated manner. Try to make characters in the story come alive for your listeners so that they will get a mental picture of the scene, situation, and players. This illusion of reality is helped by an original, straightforward introduction. Listeners yawn at hackneyed expressions like "This reminds me of a story," or "Let me illustrate my point with an anecdote I find amusing." Simply begin telling it: "Last

month the mayor of a Nevada mining town was startled to learn . . ."

This project requires a brief talk in which you develop a single point by means of anecdote. You may include either one or two anecdotes, depending upon the time, but if two are used, each should support the same point. Follow this sequence:

1. **Opening.** Just start telling the anecdote. Don't state your point.
2. **Anecdote.** While telling the anecdote(s), imply your point but don't state it.

3. Transitions. Get from the first anecdote into the second anecdote, if you have a second one. Then lead into your statement of the main point.

4. Conclusion. State your point.

Four aspects of delivery will be practiced. Directness and animation have already been introduced (see Project 7). Appearance and bodily action will be added to the Criticism Chart. Study the chart, pages 27–28, to see how these additional aspects of delivery will be judged. Try to include the appropriate details as you practice your talk aloud. Don't memorize, and don't overuse your notes.

8 CRITICISM CHART
THE SPEECH UNIT: INDUCTIVE

NAME_____ TIME_____ TO_____ TOTAL_____

TOPIC_____

Opening   1   2   3   4   5

   Began with illustration: well done—fair—weak

   Stated the point—used extraneous materials—"hemmed and hawed"

Anecdote   1   2   3   4   5

   Style: narrative—not narrative

   Details: enough—too many—too few

   Arrangement: clear, easy to follow—unclear, vague, confused; built to climax—"ran down"—
      no climax—anticlimax

   General effect: pointed, appropriate, interesting, good taste—pointless, inappropriate, insuf-
      ficiently interesting, in poor taste, tended to "drag" in places

Transitions   1   2   3   4   5

   Adequate—fair—lacking; brief—too brief; smooth, appropriate—wordy, awkward, inappro-
      priate, abrupt

Conclusion   1   2   3   4   5

   Main point: stated—not stated; clear—not clear enough; brief—too brief—wordy, abstract,
      technical, involved; appropriate—inappropriate; smooth—too abrupt

Delivery

   Directness: excellent—partial—lacking; looked at audience—looked at floor, ceiling, walls,
      out of window, over the heads, at notes, at one person or part of audience—eyes shifty,
      faraway look; general manner aloof, condescending, reserved, passive, impersonal, uncer-
      tain—friendly, poised, communicative, forceful, intense

Animation: facial expression excellent—partial—lacking—overdone—inappropriate; general manner lively, enthusiastic, alert—listless, colorless, stolid

Appearance: dress appropriate, well groomed—distracting; posture alert, at ease—tense, stiff, formal—slouchy, stooped, listless, sways, swings, leans on_____

Bodily Action:
    Platform position: no change—pacing, restless; moved about easily—awkwardly—mechanically; moved at appropriate times—at inappropriate times
    Feet: well managed—fair—distracting; jiggling, teetering—spraddled—at attention—weight one foot—shifting
    Basic hand positions: satisfactory—constantly shifted—the same; behind back—at sides—in pockets—in front of body—on lectern—twisted or rubbed together; fiddling with
_____

Gestures: lacking—seldom—frequent—too many; natural—appropriate—not carried through—lack variety

9

outlining

The purposes of this section are (1) to provide you with step-by-step procedures for building speech outlines, and (2) to provide several exercises for the practicing of these procedures.

In the two preceding projects you were introduced to the concept of a speech unit. However, in both cases you practiced short talks requiring only one speech unit. In the current project you will tackle the job of organizing a more complex and longer speech, requiring two or more main points and probably some subpoints. You will find that the same basic logic and structure of a single speech unit provides the key for coordinating several such units into a more ambitious speech design.

BACKGROUND

Speech outlining is a method of putting the ideas of a speech into a condensed written form that indicates the relationships among those ideas. Thinking is the core of outlining; the outline itself is only a written record of thought. The making of a written outline, however, helps to clarify, to test, and to preserve your thoughts.

Most speeches should have a clearly defined beginning (introduction), middle (body or discussion), and end (conclusion). Inexperienced speakers will be wise to use introduction, body, and conclusion as the three major divisions for all their speech outlines; variations should not be tried until the student has had considerable speaking experience.

The outline for the body of the speech should provide a logical hierarchy of ideas which may be visualized as a pyramid—the peak is the central idea of the speech; immediately beneath the central idea are a few main points; next, there is a layer of subpoints; and the base of the pyramid comprises details, such as facts, figures, and quotations. Each layer may be described as "supporting" the layers above it. In this hierarchy the ideas within a level are described as coordinate, and each level is said to be subordinate to the level above it. The customary mechanics for putting the hierarchy into written form are as follows:

I. Roman numerals
  A. Capital letters
    1. Arabic numerals
      a. Small letters
        (1) Arabic numerals in parentheses
          (a) Small letters in parentheses

Better outlines can be built with a minimum of wasted time if you do the job systematically and if you make that system habitual. In the next few pages we will develop a well-tried, six-step method:

1. State the central idea.
2. Choose the main points.
3. Support each main point.
4. Plan the conclusion.
5. Plan the introduction.
6. Test the transitions.

INSTRUCTIONS

stating the central idea

The central idea is a one-sentence summary of the subject matter of the entire speech. But exactly how do you go about finding, choosing, and wording a central idea?

Suppose that you are interested in rocks and minerals and that you have decided to use that interest as a topic for a brief classroom speech. (This neutral topic is deliberately chosen to provide minimum distraction from the main objective of illustrating what goes on in one's mind when systematically constructing an effective speech outline.) Suppose that you have had considerable experience with rocks and minerals, and that you have read several books and articles on the subject. Obviously you cannot cram everything you know about the subject into a few minutes. Furthermore, you would have a sadly disorganized speech if you simply jotted down five or ten minutes' worth of facts chosen at random. So you must accomplish two things: (1) Narrow the topic by focusing upon one phase or aspect; (2) Do this in a way that will facilitate the choice and arrangement of supporting materials.

You can narrow the topic "rocks and minerals" by choosing a sub-topic, such as "common rocks," "rare minerals," "how rocks are formed," "panning for gold," or the like. In addition you can guide the choice of supporting points by properly composing a complete sentence which makes a statement about the chosen subtopic. Suppose that you choose the subtopic "collecting rocks and minerals." Immediately ask yourself, "What about it?" Then find a one-sentence answer that you can develop adequately in a limited time. Word the possible sentence carefully and thoughtfully. For instance, "Collecting rocks and minerals is a fascinating hobby." But do you really want to restrict yourself to "fascinating"? That might become cloying. Perhaps "worthwhile" is the word you want. However, that might guide you into a speech which is too matter-of-fact. Suppose you try, "Collecting rocks and minerals is a desirable hobby." If this does not work out, you can go back and improve upon the wording later.

choosing the main points

The second step in the construction of an outline is to choose a set of from two to five main points. Only rarely should there be more than five, since the audience cannot ordinarily be expected to remember more than five.

The main points should be of approximately equal weight or importance; each should be stated as a complete sentence. Taken together, the main points should suffice to support your central idea. Remember that "to support" means to clarify, reinforce, or prove.

Sometimes you may create a set of main points by analyzing your central idea in terms of audience and speech purpose. Let us apply this to our example, "Collecting rocks and minerals is a desirable hobby." Do we need to clarify the statement? Probably not—most of the class will understand it well enough. Do we need to reinforce the statement? Only if audience members already believe it, but that is unlikely; most of them have probably never given the matter much thought. Therefore, you want to support the statement by proving its truth. So what makes this hobby desirable? Well, it takes people on hikes out of doors; it also provides hours of indoor relaxation studying and mounting specimens; it is inexpensive; it encourages people to learn something about geology. There we have four possible main points. Together they should suffice to prove the truth of our central idea. However, they do not seem to be of equal weight, and they do not seem to be worded properly. If we continue to think about them, juggling them around, and wording them in various ways, we may come up with a set of main headings like the following:

   I. It is enjoyable.
   II. It is inexpensive.
   III. It is instructive.

In trying to find a set of main points, you will often be stimulated by comparing your central idea with various stock speech designs. There are many patterns or sequences of main points that can be adapted to a wide variety of speech subjects and central ideas. A check list of stock designs is given on page 32.

supporting each main point

Just as the main points should support the central idea, so each main point should be supported by subpoints and details. You read the first main point, asking, "What is necessary to clarify, reinforce or prove this point?" To return to our example, the first main point was, "It [the hobby of collecting rocks and minerals] is enjoyable." Perhaps we should use two subpoints:

   A. You will enjoy hiking. (If this is true, the main point is true.)

   B. You will enjoy identifying and mounting specimens at home. (If this is true, the main point is true.)

Our second main point was, "It is inexpensive." Here we have a choice. We may go directly to forms of support regarding costs. Or we may group the costs into subpoints:

   A. You can buy the needed tools for as little as $6.

   B. You can buy a beginning book for as little as 59 cents.

The third main point was, "It is instructive." We

must be selective here for at least two reasons: (1) the point could easily be elaborated beyond our time limits, and (2) the point could be killed if we become too technical or pedantic. So we must not be too ambitious, and we must try to adapt subpoints to our listeners. Here is one possibility:

A. You [the classroom audience] will immediately acquire an unusual topic for conversation.

B. You will soon acquire some surprising information about local geology.

Now we have three pairs of subpoints, but they will not stand alone—again we must provide supports. We are ready for some details: facts, figures, and the like.

We said, "You will enjoy hiking." How to prove this? Perhaps you should tell the story of a recent hiking trip, stressing details that listeners would be likely to find interesting. As you read each of the remaining subpoints you will think of other means of support: showing them specimens of colorful or unusual rocks and minerals, quoting from one or two books, describing a few startling facts about nearby geological formations and showing how those facts influence the way of life in this community. These detailed forms of support should be specified under each subpoint, using appropriate numerals or letters to show their functions and sequence.

planning the conclusion

After you have outlined the body of the speech, you should consider plans for the speech conclusion. The simplest and most frequently used plan is simply to restate your central idea and main points, following this with a succinct statement of what you want your listeners to do or think or feel about the matter.

planning the introduction

You may have supposed that the speech opening should have been planned first, but an introduction cannot be planned until you know what you are going to introduce. So at this point you will review the outline of the body of the speech, asking yourself, "What is a good way to lead into this?"

The simplest and most common method for opening a speech is a brief statement which you think might catch the favorable attention of the audience and direct it toward your topic; then state your central idea and give a preview of your main points.

testing the transitions

At this stage it appears that we have developed a complete speech outline. We should wait, however, until we have tested the transitions. Transitions show the logical or psychological relationships among the parts of your outline. They are the verbal bridges from part to point, point to subpoint, subpoint to support. Transitions bring us back to the base where we started—thinking, the core of outlining. Therefore, stating transitions fulfills two functions: (1) During the building of the outline, it helps to test the speaker's logic; (2) During the speech delivery, it helps to show the audience what the speaker's logic is.

Test transitions by running through your first draft of an outline orally—can you move smoothly from one item to the next? A classification of transitions for speechmaking follows:

1. Connective words or phrases. Example: "Identifying rocks is enjoyable. *For instance,* suppose we want to identify this rock that I hold in my hand." (Other common transitional words and phrases:

therefore, finally, for example, likewise, on the other hand, and so on.)
2. Rhetorical questions. Example: "Why is rock hunting enjoyable? Well, it takes you out of doors . . . "
3. Repetitions. Example: "This hobby is inexpensive. It is inexpensive because so few tools are needed."
4. Perspective centered about first, second, third. Example: "Collecting rocks and minerals is a desirable hobby for three main reasons. First, it is . . . "
5. Perspective centered about speaker, audience, occasion. Example: "I [speaker] have sought to show you [audience] today [occasion] that . . . "

If you have trouble in moving orally from one item in your outline to the next item, you had better make some changes. As soon as your transitions are smooth, you are ready to commit the entire outline to written form. This has been done in the sample outline that follows; you will see how the mechanics of this written form are able to reflect the thinking that went before. Forms of support are identified in brackets.

SAMPLE OUTLINE

introduction

Here is a remarkable piece of rock—just look at it. I found this rock right here on our own campus, and there's a story behind it which I will presently tell. Maybe that story will interest you in the hobby of rock-collecting. You will discover that this hobby is enjoyable, inexpensive, and instructive. You might even make a fortune from it!

body

Central Idea: Collecting rocks and minerals is a desirable hobby.
  I. It is enjoyable.
   A. You will enjoy hiking.
      1. Last weekend two friends and I enjoyed some beautiful scenery, a mineral find, and a mild adventure with some wild animals. [Anecdote]
      2. After our return we found that we were relaxed, refreshed, and pleasantly tired. [Description]
   B. You will enjoy identifying and mounting specimens at home.
      1. Here is an interesting specimen; let's identify it together. [Visual aid; explanation]
      2. Here is a mounted collection—let me tell you about it. [Visual aid; description]
 II. It is inexpensive.
   A. You can buy the needed tools for about $6.
      1. Here is an inexpensive rock pick. [Visual aid; statistic]
      2. You probably own other necessary tools—magnifying glass, pocketknife, a penny, etc. [Instances]
   B. You can buy a beginning book for less than $1.
      1. Here is a paperback by Paul Shaffer which sells for only 59 cents. [Visual aid; statistic; perhaps read a brief quotation]
      2. Here are two longer books by Pough and by Pearl; each is authoritative; they sell for about $6 and $7. [Visual aids; statistics]
III. It is instructive.
   A. You will immediately acquire an unusual topic for conversation. [Have we time for subpoints? Or shall we just support by an anecdote?]
   B. You will soon acquire some surprising infor- about local geology.
      1. The soil is . . . [Possible supports: description, quotations]
      2. Our water supply depends upon . . . [Possible supports: now *you* supply a few appropriate possibilities]

conclusion

This morning I have sought to show that collecting rocks and minerals is a desirable hobby. It is enjoyable; it is inexpensive; it is instructive. Why not give it a try? Almost every weekend I go rock hunting. Let me invite you to come along. Maybe we'll discover a uranium treasure. More certain, and more important—we'll have a wonderful time.

STOCK SPEECH DESIGNS

1. Past, present, future (or other time sequence
2. Local, state, national, international (or other space sequence)
3. Cause, effect
4. Need, desirability, practicality, alternatives
5. Problem, solution
6. Who, what, why, when, how, where
7. Advantages, disadvantages
8. Attention, need, satisfaction, visualization, action
9. Theory, practice
10. Physical, mental, emotional, spiritual
11. Heredity, environment
12. Thinking, feeling, doing
13. Structure, function
14. Political, economic, social
15. Resemblances, differences
16. Background, characteristics, accomplishments
17. Stop, look, listen (or other catch phrase)
18. Symptoms, prevention, cure
19. Extended analogy
20. Partitioning a quotation
21. ABC's (or other letter combination)
22. Spelling a key word

---

constructing an original outline

You should now undertake to construct a speech outline of your own. In the "rocks and minerals" illustration, we sought to present a systematic, logical, and time-saving procedure. Of course the step-by-step procedure is not to be used as inflexibly as a recipe for baking a cake. But it does provide useful guidelines, a sort of "flexible formula," which, used with common sense, will improve your efficiency.

Usually one must begin with a general topic. For purposes of this project, make a list of three or four such topics on which you might wish to speak. Almost always the topic must next be narrowed in terms of your time limits and the audience's interests. Now comes a more difficult task: translating a topic into a statement of the central idea. Here you must think creatively and usually make a choice of one of several alternative ideas. Notice that a general topic, or a narrowed version of it, may be stated in a single word or phrase. By contrast the central idea must be stated as a complete sentence, and you should word this sentence with special care.

At this point, put the suggestions in the preceding paragraph into practice; use the form on page 35.

Progressing systematically, you should next practice the selection of a set of from two to five main points (remember that the word "point" is used as a technical term in speech outlining). Think carefully of your central idea vis-à-vis your audience: Is your dominant task to clarify, to reinforce, or to prove? Having answered that crucial question, you may well restudy the list of stock speech designs on page 32. Perhaps one or more of these designs can be adapted readily to your needs; if not, the list may stimulate your independent thinking. In any event, the main points should be chosen now, at least tentatively, and put into complete sentences.

Try out the above suggestions; use the form on page 37.

At this stage choose one of the topics and its design in order to practice developing a complete outline. Here you should use pages of ordinary writing paper because you may want to make corrections or other changes as you move along. To keep a perspective of the format of the final product in your mind's eye, however, take another look at the one on pages 31–32. Of course, you concentrate first on the "Body," so write the central idea at the top of a page and also the first main point. Should you support this point directly, or do you need subpoints? In either case, jot down a list of possible supports: restatements, anecdotes, and so on. (If your list is skimpy, maybe you need to do more research.) You have already practiced supporting one main point in the preceding projects on the speech unit; what you are now doing is treating each main point or subpoint as the keystone of a speech unit.

Decide next on a suitable conclusion and introduction. Probably the simplest way to do this is to write out a brief paragraph for each. (Openings and conclusions will be treated in greater detail in the next two projects.) Your instructor may request that you type or write a clean copy of your outline, to be turned in for criticism.

NAME _____ DATE _____

1. Topic:

2. Narrowing of topic:

3. Central idea:

1. Topic:

2. Narrowing of topic:

3. Central idea:

1. Topic:

2. Narrowing of topic:

3. Central idea:

1. Topic:

2. Narrowing of topic:

3. Central idea:

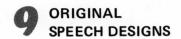

9 ORIGINAL SPEECH DESIGNS

NAME _____ DATE_____

1. Topic:

2. Central idea:

3. Set of main points:

1. Topic:

2. Central idea:

3. Set of main points:

1. Topic:

2. Central idea:

3. Set of main points:

10

forms of support

OBJECTIVE

This project will direct your attention to the materials available for clarification, reinforcement, and proof of your points. Because statements of general ideas are rarely moving, you should know the various ways to develop ideas, and you should appreciate their comparative effectiveness in adding interest, conviction, and impressiveness to your points.

BACKGROUND

Without development and confirmation, a speech would be much like the table of contents of a book, terse and starkly factual but hardly impelling. Points in a speech often need illumination or strengthening, or they may require demonstration that they are probably true. Sometimes the speech point needs all three—clarification, reinforcement, and proof. Your audience —and its knowledge and attitudes toward the subject—will largely determine the kinds and amount of supporting material needed. Ability to amplify speech ideas skillfully should be one of your aims during the study of spoken communication.

The most frequently used forms of support are:
1. **Explanation.** Development through definition, analogy, classification, or analysis.
2. **Description.** A word picture of a person, place, or event.
3. **Anecdote.** A narrative example or a brief story with a point.
4. **Instances.** An undetailed example, case, or fact, cited briefly.
5. **Quotations.** The opinion or testimony of someone else (preferably with acknowledgment of source).
6. **Statistics.** A numerical compilation of facts or particulars.
7. **Audio-visual supports.** Amplification by means of devices of sight and/or sound in addition to the sight of a speaker and the sound of his voice.

This enumeration of forms of support should not mislead you into thinking that these types are always clearly differentiated, or that points are usually developed by only one support. In actual practice you will find many excellent supporting materials that combine two or more of these methods. Your decision will depend upon how important you think the point is and how much effort you think is required to clarify, reinforce, or prove it, and the comparative interest value of your choices. Remember that a speech usually gains in clarity and vividness through an intermingling of the tools of amplification.

INSTRUCTIONS

1. Read several recent speeches from the newspapers, *Vital Speeches,* or an anthology of modern speeches— for example, one of the annual volumes of *Representative American Speeches.* Examine these speeches to discover forms of support used by speakers to clarify, reinforce, or prove their points. Choose one example of each of the following forms: explanation, description, anecdote, instances, quotation, statistics. Record these examples on the form on pages 41–42. In each case identify the speaker, his subject, and the occasion in the space indicated.

2. Prepare a three-to five-minute talk in which you will support only one or two main points. In other talks you will have an opportunity to practice several forms of support, such as description, anecdote, visual aids, and so on. This time, practice the use of statistics. You may, of course, include other forms of support if appropriate. Other suggestions:

a. Unless absolute accuracy is required, present most of your figures in round numbers. For instance, say "more than a mile high" rather than "5,398.2 feet of altitude."

b. The statistics should be clear, interesting, and dependable, with their source identified.

c. Use charts, graphs, or printed handouts if appropriate.

d. Clarify your statistics by means of at least one analogy. For example, after giving the statistics on the sizes of the sun and the planets, you might then clarify the comparative statistics by saying, "If the earth is the size of an orange, then this planet would be the size of a grapefruit, the second would be the size of a pea, the next would be the size of a medicine ball," etc.

e. Study the Criticism Chart, pages 43–44. Your instructor may wish to use it in evaluating your talk.

NAME_____ DATE_____

1. Speaker, subject, occasion:

Example of "explanation":

2. Speaker, subject, occasion:

Example of "description":

3. Speaker, subject, occasion:

Example of "anecdote":

4. Speaker, subject, occasion:

    Example of "instances":

5. Speaker, subject, occasion:

    Example of "quotation":

6. Speaker, subject, occasion:

    Example of "statistics":

NAME_____ TIME_____ TO_____TOTAL_____

TOPIC_____

Content

    Speech structure   1 2 3 4 5

      Suggestions:

   Statistics   1 2 3 4 5

Did they support a main point?	Yes	Partly	No
Were they impressive?	Yes	Partly	No
Were they clearly understandable?	Yes	Partly	No
Were they easily remembered?	Yes	Partly	No

Analogies   1 2 3 4 5

Did they explain the statistics?	Yes	Partly	No
Were they appropriate?	Yes	Partly	No
Were they vivid?	Yes	Partly	No

Delivery   1   2   3   4   5

Directness:

Animation:

Physical appearance:

Posture:

Bodily action:

Voice and articulation:

11

speech openings

OBJECTIVE

The opening words can sometimes make or break the entire speech. Therefore the ways of opening a talk deserve a more detailed study than was possible in previous assignments. In this section you will consider the functions of the introduction and ways of accomplishing these functions. Although the introduction comes first in your speech, it usually is prepared last—after you have considered the audience and the direction of your remarks to them.

BACKGROUND

The very fact that the opening words of a talk provide the listeners' first impressions of your speech gives those words psychological significance. If you do not secure favorable attention at the beginning of a speech, it may be hard to do it later. And, of course, if you fail to catch audience attention at first, it makes little difference what you say. Or if you begin by antagonizing or confusing the audience, your hope of winning favorable response becomes pretty dim. Of course some spokesmen for minority views may find it so difficult to secure any kind of hearing that they deliberately do antagonize their audiences. In these extreme cases, the speaker takes a calculated risk in trading favorable response for attention, and the tactic may boomerang.

The purposes of a speech introduction are three: (1) to arouse favorable attention; (2) to promote friendliness and respect; (3) to lead into the subject. Getting positive attention is the first concern of any speaker. Often you must overcome audience inertia or distraction, but this must be done without creating antipathy. For example, a talk begun with a belch probably would attract audience attention to the speaker, but the attention would scarcely be favorable. The speech opening seeks more than favorable attention; it also tries to earn a friendly attitude toward the speaker as a person. In those first few moments, you want to earn respect and good will. Audiences quickly assess the the speaker's personal warmth and sincerity; while the listeners may alter their opinions later, they do receive an initial impression that will either help or hinder the speaker. A third aim must be achieved during the beginning of your speech. You must lead into your subject and reveal the direction the speech is going to take. What is the best way to approach the speech theme in order to accomplish its purpose? Much of this decision will be determined by the attitude of the audience toward your subject. A friendly audience will permit you to get into the subject more quickly than a hostile one, while an indifferent audience may require deliberate arousal of curiosity and stimulation of interest. Preliminary audience analysis will guide your selection of the most appropriate introductory remarks.

Keeping in mind the three functions of a speech introduction, we can list the most frequently successful ways of opening a talk:

1. Reference to previous speaker or chairman
2. Reference to occasion
3. Honest compliment to audience
4. Appropriate joke or other humor
5. Unison audience reaction: show of hands, singing, applause
6. Statement of central idea or purpose
7. Startling statement
8. Thought-provoking quotation
9. Illustrative anecdote
10. Establishment of common ground
11. Series of rhetorical questions
12. Personal reference
13. Reference to recent event
14. Visual aids
15. Definition of terms
16. Reference to importance of subject

The introduction may consist of just one of the above ingredients; more often, however, it consists of a combination of two or more. When a combination is attempted, the ingredients usually are blended rather than simply strung in sequence. The resultant introduction should become an integral part of the whole speech—not a tacked-on prelude or preface, but one of its essential functions.

INSTRUCTIONS

1. Read several recent speeches from the sources given on page 39. Using the form on page 47, write in full or paraphrase a sample of opening remarks that exemplifies an effective introduction. Identify the speaker, his audience, and give the gist of his subsequent remarks.

2. Using the form on page 49, write out as fully as possible the opening that you would use for a given audience, topic, and central idea.

3. Using the form on page 51, describe a subject and central idea that you might use for some future classroom speech. In the space provided, briefly outline the possible opening remarks. Be prepared to speak to the class using these notes. If your instructor asks you to give this introductory portion of a speech to the class, you will be judged on three bases: Did you capture class attention? Did you establish a friendly attitude toward yourself as a person? Did you lead into your central idea? An overall test of your effectiveness might be this: having heard these opening remarks, how many members of the class would like to hear the rest of the speech? These criticisms may be recorded on pages 51–52.

11 OPENING REMARKS FROM A PUBLISHED SPEECH

NAME_____ DATE _____

Source:

Name of speaker:

Date of speech:

Place where speech was delivered:

Brief description of the audience:

Nature of the occasion:

Brief summary of the body of the speech:

The speech opening (verbatim, summary in student's words, or a combination of these two ways of reporting):

NAME _____ DATE _____

Proposed topic:

Proposed audience and occasion:

Proposed central idea:

Proposed speech opening (verbatim or nearly so):

NAME _____ DATE_____

Topic:

Central idea:

Speaking notes for the opening:

Critique of the opening remarks (if they were actually delivered):

NOTE: Any of several methods may be used to secure ratings by the class on the following questions.

1. To what extent did the opening arouse favorable attention?

2. To what extent did the opening create friendly attitudes toward the speaker?

3. To what extent did the opening effectively lead into the central idea of the proposed speech?

4. How many members of the class would honestly like to hear the rest of this speech?

12

speech conclusions

OBJECTIVE

In the closing moments of a talk you have one final chance to ensure the success of the entire speech. Some preliminary suggestions regarding speech conclusions were given in Project 9. Now we need to explore this matter in greater detail. What are the functions of a speech conclusion? What are some of the methods for concluding a talk effectively?

BACKGROUND

Someone has said that there are just three rules for a public speaker: "Stand up, speak up, and shut up." But this advice, if followed literally, often has unpleasant results. A speaker sometimes ends his speech abruptly, leaving the listeners expectant and dissatisfied; the speech seems unfinished. Or the speaker may grope his way toward an ending, concluding with a lame statement: "Well, I guess that's about all I have to say, so I guess I'd better stop now." Either of these makeshift endings will dampen the impact of an otherwise effective presentation. Good conclusions impart a sense of completeness to the speech and end it on a note of finality.

The purpose of the conclusion is to bring the entire speech into focus on its central idea; all that you have said should be drawn together in the conclusion to add a final impetus to your main idea. The conclusion gives you an opportunity to condense your message into an easily remembered unit and place it squarely in the center of listener attention. It is the capstone of your remarks. To accomplish this purpose the conclusion must be planned and phrased carefully. Effective conclusions seldom are improvised during the delivery of a speech, and they rarely arise from inspirations of the moment.

Three types of conclusion will serve most purposes: (1) a summary that swiftly touches the high points of the speech; (2) an appeal that identifies your speech with the desires and aspirations of your listeners; (3) a call for action that enlists audience support for your proposition. These ways of concluding may be used singly or in combination. Their effectiveness is often enhanced by means of the following rhetorical devices:
1. Enumeration
2. Restatement
3. Quotation
4. Climactic anecdote
5. Rhetorical question
6. Epigram or proverb
7. Prophecy
8. Personal reference
9. Challenge

A good conclusion uses one or more of these devices to place before the audience, sharply and interestingly, the essence of a speech. Like the introduction and body of a speech, it is planned beforehand and made an integral part of the outline. Speech conclusions can vary greatly in length. Sometimes the point of a whole speech can be distilled into a single concluding sentence; at other times, many sentences may be required. Conclusions average about 5 percent of the length of most talks. Whatever their length, they should represent what educator and popular lecturer Harry Overstreet termed "the delightful art of closing with a snap."

INSTRUCTIONS

1. By this time you should already have read several recent published speeches. Choose one which you think might illustrate the functions and methods of concluding a talk. Describe this speech and record its closing remarks as indicated on the form on pages 55–56. On the second part of this form give your critical opinions of the speech conclusion.

2. Using the form on page 57, state the central idea and describe the design of a proposed classroom talk that you might give. Then write the proposed conclusion in full. You will probably be asked by your instructor to read this material in front of the class. If he then provides a method by which you will receive criticism from the class, fill out the other part of the form, page 58, in the light of such criticism.

NAME _____ DATE _____

Source:

Name of speaker:

Date of speech:

Place where speech was delivered:

Brief description of audience:

Nature of the occasion:

Brief summary of the body of the speech:

The speech conclusion (verbatim, summary in student's words, or a combination of these two ways of reporting):

Critique:

1. What was the conclusion type (summary, emotional appeal, or call for action)?

2. What rhetorical devices were used?

3. Was the conclusion appropriate to the speech, speaker, occasion?

4. Was the conclusion probably effective with this audience?

5. Was the conclusion too short or too long?

6. Can you think of any way to improve upon the conclusion?

12 PROPOSED CONCLUSION FOR ORIGINAL SPEECH

NAME _____ DATE _____

Central idea:

Brief summary of speech design or body of speech:

Proposed conclusion (write it in full):

Critique:

1. What type of conclusion were you attempting to use?

2. What rhetorical devices did you try to use?

3. How effective was the conclusion in terms of class response?

4. Having tried it before the class, can you now think of any ways of improving this speech conclusion?

13

language and style

OBJECTIVE

In this section we are concerned with sharpening your awareness of the importance of word choice and composition. Much of the effectiveness of your speeches depends upon compositional skill—the selection and management of verbal symbolism. A speaker's effortless employment of accurate, colorful, and varied language inevitably heightens audience attention and understanding. Clumsy, thoughtless composition just as surely deadens the impact of a speech.

BACKGROUND

Matthew Arnold once said that the secret of style was to have something to say and to say it as clearly as you can. The advice is excellent for any public speaker, since communication of ideas, the aim of speech-making, involves both content and its transmission to listeners. Although there is no infallible guide to good speech style, we know that effective language is clear, interesting, and appropriate. Each speaker should ask himself honestly: Am I successful in making myself understood? Does my speech seem to invite and hold attention? Does my language meet standards of acceptable usage? Does it help listeners remember and accept my ideas?

The speaker's thoughts become clear only as they are translated into appropriate words in meaningful combinations. Thus sentences should be constructed carefully so that ideas are received as you intend them to be understood. Don't blame your "ignorant audience" for its inability to follow a haphazardly composed speech. But vivid words and expressions, well-chosen figures of speech, concrete terminology, originality—all make thoughts cut deeply. Variety in the length and complexity of sentences helps sustain attention. In general, speakers should:

Prefer the familiar word to the technical
Prefer the concrete word to the abstract
Prefer the direct word to the circumlocution
Prefer the vivid word to the noncommittal
Prefer the specific word to the general
Prefer the unusual word to the trite

Audiences naturally downgrade a speaker who uses crude grammar. They also discount a speech speckled with meaningless, though grammatically correct, expressions. Clichés such as the following usually are only verbal fillers: "last but not least," "see what I mean?" "like," "you know," "and so forth and so on," "the one and only," "in other words," "without further ado." Such trite phrases dilute the impact of a speech, and when used repeatedly stamp the speaker as unoriginal and careless. Have you ever become so engrossed in counting the times a speaker used a pet expression that you stopped listening to his thoughts?

The improving speaker will strengthen his language through systematic, varied reading of good literature, including notable speeches. References such as *Composing the Speech* by Glen Mills, *A Sense of Style* by Jane Blankenship, and G. P. Morhmann's *Composition and Style for the Public Speaker* are valuable because of their extensive treatment of the language and style of public speaking. Notice, as you read and listen, the differences between written and oral style: speech style makes greater use of interpolations, asides, editorial comments, personal pronouns in the first or second person, interrogatives, contractions, broken sentences, and repetition. But though the language of written prose differs somewhat from good oral style, familiarity with good literature challenges you to improve your own standards of composition; the reading of good speeches shows you what can be done with the language of speech. *Roget's Thesaurus*, with its remarkable array of synonyms, and an up-to-date dictionary, to provide a record of current usage, belong on every speaker's bookshelf. Your goal is not the achievement of self-conscious "purple patches," but rather the effortless use of the simple, expressive language that marks effective speech composition.

INSTRUCTIONS

1. Find a portion of a recent published speech that illustrates superior, attention-holding composition. Bring your selection to class to read aloud. What ingredients of good style contribute to its effectiveness?

2. Following a regular assigned speech, have some other class member paraphrase the talk. Discuss variations or discrepancies between the listeners' summaries and the speaker's intended meaning. Where did the speaker fail to communicate? Or the listener miss the point?

3. For this portion of the assignment you will find six examples of poor composition; then you will revise them. Each excerpt will exemplify fuzzy meaning; each will be from a published speech or other written source; each will be about twenty-five words in length. Rewrite each passage so as to improve upon its clarity and accuracy. Use the form on pages 61–62 for this exercise. Why not try to choose one of your bad examples from the text of this guidebook?

4. Read several speeches in a collection of notable speeches in the English language (Baird, *American Public Addresses,* McBath and Fisher, *British Public Addresses, 1828–1960,* etc.). Select one speech for comment on style in terms of the recommendations presented in this section. Can you find excerpts to illustrate your comments?

Source:

Excerpt:

Revision:

Source:

Excerpt:

Revision:

Source:

Excerpt:

Revision:

Source:

Excerpt:

Revision:

Source:

Excerpt:

Revision:

Source:

Excerpt:

Revision:

14

vocabulary

OBJECTIVE

There is today a growing realization that a student's mastery of words is related to his development of executive and leadership potential, and that it is to some extent an index of IQ and general intellectual ability.

The purposes of this section are (1) to draw attention to the study of words, and (2) to direct you to ways of enlarging and enriching your vocabulary.

BACKGROUND

The English language contains more than half a million words, but in ordinary speaking you use only a small percentage of them. Thus you have ample room for building a larger and better vocabulary. A rich vocabulary provides you with apt alternatives, not to dazzle an audience, but to enable you to select instantaneously the most suitable vehicle for conveying your thoughts.

One of the best methods for improving vocabulary is reading, especially *oral* reading, of the works of authors and speakers who are recognized masters of style. You should alert yourself to notice unfamiliar words, to look them up in the dictionary for their meanings, and to practice using them until their use becomes natural to you. Many speakers resolve to use at least three new words in each speech they give. Command of a word requires that you know at least the following about it: (1) its spelling, (2) its pronunciation, (3) its definition and meaning, (4) its acceptable usage, and (5) how it sounds when you use it orally.

INSTRUCTIONS

1. Your instructor may wish to conduct a definition bee or pronunciation bee. If so, the class will be divided into two or more teams. Exact rules for judging and scoring, similar to those of the old familiar spelling bees, will be agreed upon in advance. The instructor will provide lists of "words every public speaker should know," and contestants will vie at defining them. Or he may provide lists of commonly mispronounced words, and each team will try to score the highest number of correct pronunciations.

2. Most of you are familiar with the long-time *Reader's Digest* feature on enriching your word power.

The following vocabulary test contains sixty words drawn from this stimulating and useful series. Take the test, circling the letter before the best choice, then examine the correct answers and their derivation. Don't peek at answers in the Appendix. Use the quiz as a helpful check on the strength of your word power.

3. Try the following test on synonyms. Read each sentence thoughtfully; then choose the best word or phrase among the alternatives offered to fill the blank space. Indicate your choice by circling the letter preceding your chosen item. Answers will be found in the Appendix.

vocabulary test

The items in this test were drawn from the original series, "It Pays to Increase Your Word Power." Reprinted by special permission of the *Reader's Digest*.

1. cogent a: brief. b: wise. c: convincing. d: mathematical term.
2. amelioration a: pleasure. b: act of apologizing. c: improvement. d: humiliation.
3. ferment a: heat. b: decay. c: power. d: agitation.
4. ambient a: sufficient. b: circular. c: moving around. d: complete.
5. cursory a: informal. b: penetrating. c: angry. d: rapid and superficial.
6. recapitulate a: to recover property. b: sum up. c: repeat oneself tiresomely. d: surrender again.
7. polemical a: controversial. b: pertaining to electrical poles. c: eloquent. d: scholarly.
8. conjecture a: exclamation. b: argument. c: positive statement. d: judgment based on incomplete evidence.
9. sophistry a: wisdom. b: ignorance. c: wit. d: tricky argumentation.
10. circumlocution a: grammatical error. b: rambling. c: roundabout way of talking. d: prudence.
11. refute a: to reprove sharply. b: disprove. c: insult. d: disapprove.
12. promulgation a: proclamation. b: advocacy. c: invention. d: imposition upon others.
13. anomalous a: homeless. b: nameless. c: deviating from the common rule. d: perplexing.
14. espouse a: to explain. b: advocate. c: expose. d: claim.
15. *quid pro quo* a: puzzle. b: something for nothing. c: proposition. d: one thing in return for another.
16. capricious a: cute. b: flirtatious. c: vain. d: fickle.
17. redoubtable a: blameless. b: untrustworthy. c: formidable. d: reckless.
18. equivocate a: to be fair-minded. b: say one thing and mean another. c: be witty. d: be undecided.
19. probity a: proof. b: curiosity. c: taste. d: strict honesty.
20. arrogate a: to brag. b: question. c: take or claim presumptuously. d: insult.
21. *sine qua non* a: something indispensable. b: crime. c: achievement. d: absent.

22. portentous a: ominous. b: lacking in humor. c: important. d: extremely heavy.
23. malign a: to complain of. b: swindle. c: slander. d: sicken.
24. mendicant a: wise man. b: doctor. c: wandering tribe. d: beggar.
25. encomium a: speech. b: disapproval. c: apology. d: high praise.
26. exigent a: exciting. b: urgent. c: hateful. d: mistaken.
27. vociferous a: talkative. b: enthusiastic. c: making a loud outcry. d: poisonous.
28. desultory a: without method or aim. b: despairing. c: shabby. d: lonely.
29. quixotic a: fickle. b: amusing. c: overdressed. d: unpractical.
30. verbiage a: wordiness. b: emptiness. c: bragging. d: foliage.
31. euphony a: good humor. b: pride. c: pleasing sounds. d: sense of well-being.
32. elusive a: clear. b: baffling. c: swift. d: false.
33. subvert a: to humiliate oneself. b: be abnormal. c: undermine. d: be weak.
34. quintessence a: overfussiness. b: good taste. c: purest part. d: vanity.
35. retrospection a: survey of past events. b: depression. c: interest directed toward oneself. d: investigation.
36. animus a: vulgarity. b: enthusiasm. c: hatred. d: ambition.
37. devolve a: to implicate. b: expose. c: be handed down d: spread.
38. vicissitude a: lack of decision. b: change of fortune. c: danger. d: misfortune.
39. honorarium a: promotion. b: fee for services. c: honorary college degree. d: formal speech.
40. dolorous a: dank. b: lazy. c: foolish. d: sad.
41. imputed a: revealed. b: ascribed or attributed. c: assailed. d: purged.
42. illusive a: invisible. b: imaginative. c: tending to slip away. d: deceptive and misleading.
43. nascent a: decaying. b: unpleasant in disposition. c: evil-smelling. d: starting to develop.
44. immure a: to make calm. b: sink. c: enclose within walls. d: oppose.

45. fortuitous a: sudden. b: chance. c: rash. d: courageous.
46. invidious a: deceptive. b: malicious. c: hypercritical. d: stealthy.
47. cortege a: carriage. b: procession. c: nosegay. d: close-fitting undergarment.
48. ennui a: laziness. b: worldly wisdom. c: delay. d: boredom.
49. canard a: game bird. b: false story. c: explosion. d: vase.
50. insidious a: of doubtful origin. b: secret. c: serious. d: designed to entrap.
51. salient a: smooth. b: difficult. c: outstanding. d: curved.
52. aphorism a: overornate speech. b: inoffensive expression. c: positive statement. d: maxim.
53. efficacious a: producing the desired result. b: artificial. c: fussy. d: worn-out.
54. exorcise a: to practice. b: curse. c: train for health. d: drive out.
55. controvert a: to turn around. b: attempt to disprove. c: convince. d: confuse.

56. digress a: decline to a worse state. b: make a mistake. c: lie. d: stray from the main theme.
57. spectral a: invisible. b: ghostly. c: dark. d: infinitely small.
58. captious a: fault-finding. b: insecure. c: changeable. d: vain.
59. averse a: cross. b: reluctant. c: unfortunate. d: in the opposite order.
60. saturnine a: ugly. b: threatening in manner. c: sarcastic. d: gloomy.

Now turn to the Appendix and read it carefully. As you proceed, check the items you missed. Then count the number you got right and enter your score here:

_____

Evaluation of your score:
51–60 correct   excellent
41–50 correct   good
31–40 correct   fair
below 31   buy a good dictionary immediately

SYNONYMS TEST

1. This is a test of your ability to choose the most ____ word rather than an approximate word. a. precise b. persuasive c. poetic d. impressive
2. The presidency requires more than intelligence; it requires ____. a. shrewdness b. prudence c. wisdom d. sapience
3. When policemen administer "the third degree," it means that they ____ their victim. a. hector b. cross-examine c. heckle d. chivy
4. Because "very" is an overworked word, John F. Kennedy used it with ____. a. reservation b. paucity c. restraint d. care
5. During this election campaign my opponent has tried in vain to ____ my argument. a. denounce b. disapprove c. disagree with d. refute
6. ____ is a dangerous form of humor because it may insult some of your listeners. a. wit b. irony c. sarcasm d. exaggeration
7. And now the Congressman has been forced to ____ that his tax proposal will be defeated on the House floor. a. avow b. concede c. confess d. acknowledge
8. And now the Congressman has been forced to ____ that during the past few years he has twice been arrested for reckless driving. a. avow b. concede c. confess d. acknowledge.
9. In his "Blood, Sweat and Tears" speech Winston Churchill called on the British people to ____ the bombings and other cruelties of Hitler. a. endure b. tolerate c. suffer d. abide

10. The job of a motion picture stuntman is a ____ one. a. dangerous b. hazardous c. perilous d. risky
11. Fear is ____ turned inside out. a. cowardice b. courage c. anger d. caution
12. Although we may be deceived by it, most of us are amused by ____. a. humbug b. fraud c. counterfeit d. imposture
13. It is disconcerting to a speaker when his audience remains ____. a. inactive b. passive c. inert d. supine
14. The ____ quality of country living has appeal for the harried urbanite. a. rural b. rustic c. bucolic e. pastoral
15. In a single raid in World War II, Allied bombers ____ most of Dresden, Germany. a. ravaged b. devastated c. pillaged d. despoiled
16. Presenting listeners with too many options will tend to ____ them. a. nonplus b. puzzle c. perplex d. confound
17. Voters usually will ____ officeholders who are unresponsive to public opinion. a. oust b. dismiss c. evict d. expel
18. Persuasive argument often causes listeners to ____ their beliefs. a. relinquish b. abandon c. modify d. surrender
19. The astronauts' first moon exploration was an important ____ in American history a. event b. episode c. occurrence d. incident

20. Futurists are concerned with the ____ of the year 2000. a. outlook b. foretaste c. anticipation d. prospect
21. Deliberately insulting behavior will often ____ others. a. excite b. stimulate c. provoke d. pique
22. Through his leadership ability, Franklin Roosevelt ____ the respect of men of all parties. a. procured b. obtained c. earned d. secured
23. Senators sometimes filibuster in order to ____ the passage of legislation. a. hinder b. block c. impede d. obstruct
24. It is a ____ to believe that world peace is easily achieved. a. mirage b. delusion c. illusion d. hallucination
25. Many audience members hold ____ that are difficult to change because they are strongly and seriously held. a. convictions b. impressions c. opinions d. views
26. The class was ____ by the loud noise in the corridor. a. shocked b. stupified c. stunned d. startled
27. A thrifty farmer buys his seed and fertilizer in ____. a. mass b. volume c. bulk d. magnitude
28. The knight's ____ bearing bespoke his royal training. a. proud b. arrogant c. haughty d. insolent
29. The master criminal was ____ for his exploits. a. renowned b. eminent c. celebrated d. notorious
30. Hitler's attack on Russia was a military ____. a. error b. blunder c. lapse d. mistake
31. The process of speech communication may be divided into the following ____: speech, speaker, audience, and occasion. a. elements b. ingredients c. components d. parts
32. This man is ____; he isn't even capable of loyalty. a. false b. treacherous c. traitorous d. perfidious
33. When the Salvation Army worker begins making a speech on the street corner, a crowd soon ____. a. congregates b. gathers c. assembles d. collects.
34. We embark on a long crusade; the journey will be ____. a. hard b. difficult c. arduous d. rough
35. These bureaucrats today are merely ____ but if we give them an inch, they will soon take a mile. a. impertinent b. meddlesome c. officious d. insolent

36. The great teacher ____ ideas in the minds of students who may not appreciate his greatness until years after graduation. a. instills b. inculcates c. inseminates d. implants
37. Mass media communication is sometimes divided into three main parts: a message source, a channel, and a receiver. The job of the speaker is to ____ these three parts. a. link b. connect c. unite d. combine
38. But our citizens must always ____ for themselves the rights guaranteed by the United States Constitution. a. keep b. retain c. reserve d. withhold
39. The problem is urgent; our great party ____ a leader. a. needs b. lacks c. is in want of d. requires
40. Despite all of these criticisms and attacks, I can and will ____ my position. a. maintain b. defend c. vindicate d. justify
41. "The shooting of the hunters was terrible," is an ____ sentence. a. ambiguous b. abstruse c. obscure d. enigmatic
42. In this strike we must remember that some of the union complaints are reasonable. Therefore, our task is to ____. a. pacify b. subdue c. appease d. conciliate
43. ____ upon the meaning of that concept so that you may understand it fully and deeply. a. ruminate b. meditate c. muse d. ponder
44. The artist, moved by the spirit of the moment, reacted in an ____ manner. a. indigenous b. automatic c. impulsive d. instinctive
45. The Secretary of Labor described the ____ of steel workers after their recent strike. a. state b. status c. situation d. condition
46. Officials of concentration camps systematically intimidated prisoners in order to ____ them. a. discipline b. teach c. instruct d. train
47. The girl offered a sincere ____ for striking the pedestrian. a. excuse b. apology c. alibi d. pretext
48. Clarence Darrow was famed for his ____ of the rights of the underdog. a. support b. advocacy c. backing d. championing

15

audience analysis

OBJECTIVE

Projects were provided at the beginning of this guidebook to help you get acquainted with your classmates, since they are your most usual audience this term. Now we must broaden our thinking to include other future audiences. We want to know how to gather information about other kinds of audiences and how to use that information in speechmaking.

BACKGROUND

How can you gather information about an audience? By observation and by inquiry. Suppose you are asked to address the local PTA. You can often observe them beforehand by attending a meeting—you can get a fairly accurate idea of the size of the group, composition by sex, range of ages, and so on. You can get additional information by inquiring. Ask questions of the person who invited you to speak; ask questions of other members of the group; if the group has a published newsletter or magazine, read it. Use the telephone; use correspondence.

What kind of information do you need? Study the check list on pages 70–71.

How should you use audience information in speechmaking? In general, the answer is: *adapt.* More specifically, you can adapt to an audience in at least four ways: (1) slanting the subject; (2) selecting the supports; (3) modifying the delivery; and (4) preventing blunders.

Slanting the subject. Knowledge of your audience will help you to select or narrow a topic, state the central idea, and plan the speech design. Compare, for example, a men's club with a women's club. Despite the advent of "women's lib," the findings of a research study done several years ago probably still hold true: in general, men tend to be interested in sports, business, money, politics, news events; women are more interested in home, health, personalities, clothes, social affairs. In a group where the sexes are about equally re-presented, women are more likely to adapt to men's interests than vice versa.

Selecting the supports. To continue our example, explanation and statistics might be most suitable for a men's club; the same point, however, might be better supported by description and anecdote for a women's club. If you need to use an anecdote, a story about a football game might be best for the men's audience; one about a bridge game might be better adapted to a women's audience.

Modifying delivery. In planning your delivery—both verbal and nonverbal—audience data will help. Mentally compare two different audiences, and ask yourself questions about adapting your delivery. Should you be lively or restrained? Formal or informal? Loud at times or consistently quiet? Slangy or academic? And so on.

Preventing blunders. One slip of the tongue can sometimes ruin a speech. So be especially careful to get information about race, politics, and religion. If it is known that there is even one priest, rabbi, or minister in the audience, that fact may eliminate an anecdote that you would otherwise tell. If you are speaking to an audience of divided political affiliations, you might easily make a statement that would be simultaneously applauded and booed; by wording the point more carefully, you might get applause from Democrats and Republicans alike.

INSTRUCTIONS

Make a careful study of a non-classroom audience and record your findings on the check list which begins below. Data on some of the items can be recorded by underscoring the appropriate words; for other items make notations in the blank spaces. Notice that most of this list deals with what are sometimes called "situational variables" and that most of these variables are nonverbal. Your instructor will probably want to provide additional instructions.

Meanwhile, prepare a three-minute talk on the topic "How to Lose Friends and Alienate People." For this talk you will draw upon your past observations or experience. Slant this talk to illustrate (in reverse) one or more of the principles or techniques of audience analysis and adaptation.

GUIDE SHEET FOR ANALYZING AN AUDIENCE

The Occasion

1. *Date and hour*
   Anything unusual about the date—holiday, anniversary, or such?
   Anything unusual about the hour?
2. *Attendance*
   Size of audience?
   Is attendance required or voluntary?
3. *Place of meeting*
   Outdoors or indoors?
   Shape and size of room or auditorium?
   What kind of seating arrangements?
   Speaker's platform?
   Lectern or table?
   Any stage props—water pitcher, flag, map, gavel, blackboard?
   Any room decorations?
   What kind of lighting?
   Heating and ventilation?
   Any acoustical problems—sound-deadened, echoes, public address system, competing noises?
   Are there facilities for showing slides or motion pictures?
4. *Type of meeting*
   Regular or special?
   Who is sponsoring the meeting?
   What is the purpose of the meeting?
   What is likely to be the general atmosphere, or mood, or tone?
5. *Type of program*
   Who planned the program?
   Is there a printed program?
   What will precede and follow your talk—other speakers, music, refreshments, an open forum?

Common Traits and Interests

1. *Age:* children, adolescents, young adults, middle-aged adults, old people, mixed
2. *Sex:* all men, mostly men, all women, mostly women, approximately equal
3. *Race:* black, white, Chicano or other ethnic group, mixed
4. *Family status:* single, married, parents, children
5. *Economic status:* wealthy, well-to-do, middle bracket, poor, destitute, mixed
6. *Educational status:* grammar school, high school, college, mixed
7. *Community:* farm, small town, small city, big city, mixed
8. *Occupation:* big business, small business, professional, trade, housewives, students, retired, etc.

9. *Religion:* Protestants, Catholics, Jews, other denominations, freethinkers; regular members, occasional attendance, seldom or never attend; mixtures
10. *Politics:* Republican–liberal or conservative; Democrat–liberal or conservative; independent; radical; third party; mixed
11. *Memberships:* lodges, fraternities or sororities, clubs, labor unions
12. *Entertainments:* favorite radio-TV programs, movies, dancing, athletic events, hobbies, games
13. *Sources of information:* books, magazines, newspapers, lectures, acknowledged authorities

Attitudes Toward Your Topic

1. *Favorable,* strongly or moderately
2. *Opposed,* strongly or moderately
3. *Undecided,* passively neutral or actively conflicting
4. *Indifferent,* uninformed or simply uninterested

Attitudes Toward You

1. In what respects are you like or unlike most of your audience?
   (See list of traits and interests above: age, sex, race, etc.)
2. Will the audience know in advance about these resemblances and differences?
3. What are your personal reasons for speaking here?
4. Will the audience know these reasons?
5. How many of them are personally acquainted with you?
6. Will most of them be favorably inclined toward you personally or will they be prejudiced against you?
   How will you rate on "credibility"?
   a. Will your appearance be a help or handicap?
   b. Will your voice be a help or handicap?
   c. Will your personality and usual speaking style be helps or handicaps?
   d. Will your reputation, rank or title be a help or handicap?

16

heckling

OBJECTIVE

This project will give you a chance to practice immediate adaptation to audience feedback. It will provide a revealing cross section of some of the thoughts that run through listeners' minds while they listen to a speaker.

BACKGROUND

The concept of "feedback" in the physical sciences and engineering was proposed and thoroughly developed in Norbert Wiener's landmark book *Cybernetics* (1948). Subsequently, the feedback principle has been widely applied to describe the give-and-take that characterizes the human process of communication. In a heckling talk the operation of feedback is dramatized.

As you progress in the practice of spoken communication, you become increasingly aware of the signs by which the members of your audience reveal their reactions to your speech. You realize that your listeners are mentally talking back to you, and that you can often "hear" them with your eyes—you see them smile, frown, look puzzled, nod or shake their heads, whisper, yawn, or squirm. They may laugh or applaud. Sometimes they speak back to you aloud and even boo or heckle. In all such instances you should try to adapt your mood, your manner, and your ideas to these immediate responses. (You may sometimes have to fight back; adapting to an audience does not mean surrendering.) But an effective speaker cannot afford to be unaware of them; he cannot afford to ignore them.

In this country, the listeners in most speech situations tend to repress their reactions; heckling is usually considered impolite. By contrast, in Great Britain heckling is considered normal response to political or other speeches of persuasion. British university debaters visiting in the United States often complain about the lack of give-and-take between themselves and their American audiences. The British students believe that learning when and how to reply to hecklers is an essential part of the training of a public speaker. They believe that audible comments and questions from the audience help to combat dullness, force the speaker to choose his words and ideas more carefully, and constantly remind the speaker that communication is a two-way rather than a one-way process.

INSTRUCTIONS

Prepare a two-minute talk on a subject toward which some of your listeners will be antagonistic. During the presentation of these talks, audience members will be permitted to heckle the speakers. Each student speaker will have a student chairman, and the heckling will be conducted in accordance with previously agreed rules, enforced by the student chairman. Maximum total time, including the heckling, should be about five minutes.

Following is an example of one workable set of rules: (1) A member of the audience may interrupt the speaker at any time by raising his hand and calling, "Mr. Chairman"; (2) If the Chair nods approval, the heckler asks a question or makes a comment; (3) The speaker either answers or refuses to answer, and then continues his speech; (4) The Chair may declare a moratorium on heckling if he feels that interruptions have become too frequent.

SUGGESTED TOPICS

I came here from the greatest state in the Union.

Most of you were spoiled by your overindulgent parents.

Communism is more efficient than democracy.

Taxes (or tuition) should be increased.

Our football team doesn't deserve to win a game.

Shakespeare's plays were written by someone else.

Women are inferior to men. (Or vice versa.)

The grades being given in this school are too high.

This country is not fit for world leadership.

College admission today is too easy.

Single people should be taxed higher than married ones. (Or vice versa.)

Movies are better than ever.

three

nonverbal communication

A good way to enjoy TV commercials is to turn off the sound and watch the video. What you see is often comical but always instructive.

Undistracted by the verbal patter, you can judge the effect, if any, of those whiter teeth, latest hairdos, and revolutionary new cosmetics. How much is the actor able to tell you by facial expression alone? Pay special attention to the language of gesture and bodily movement—you should be able to see the differences between the novice and the old pro as you compare a few of these sales artists. The stage sets deserve at least passing notice (if they weren't there, you would notice, indeed). Evaluate the use or overuse of other visual aids—the succession of attractive bottles, shining cars, refrigerators, clothing, bathroom fixtures, and mouth-watering plates of food, plus the cute children, dogs, and sexy-looking girls. The sudden advent of these enormously expensive electronic visual "miracles" drastically altered the social functions of the slightly older "new" media of radio, movies, and picture magazines.

You probably do not plan to become a professional performer, but the ubiquitous TV screen, the radio, and the phonograph should become laboratory equipment as you study the nonverbal, as well as the verbal, characteristics of effective everyday speech communication.

17

action talk

OBJECTIVE

When nonverbal communication is mentioned, most people think of body movements or perhaps "the language of gestures." So we will start with that.

This assignment will illustrate the fact that bodily action is not mere decoration but is an integral part of effective oral communication. You will practice to combine the audible and the visible elements of speech so that each effectively supplements the other.

BACKGROUND

Your next classroom talk will begin before you utter a word. It will begin when you rise and walk to the front of the room. The *first* impressions the audience gets are visual ones—your appearance, dress, manner of walking, facial expression, posture. Likewise, the *final* impressions are visual: after you have said the last word, you walk back to your seat.

During a talk some beginning speakers stand immobile on one spot as though rooted there; others release suppressed energy through random movements—jiggling, teetering, pacing, fiddling with a pencil or a set of notes. In this class you will practice developing habits of purposive bodily action. Some audience reactions to a speaker arise from small, barely discernible signs on his part, such as a lifted eyebrow, a slight shrug, or simply muscular tension. Other audience impressions are gained from the speaker's use of larger, more obvious bodily actions. You should first learn how to make the larger gestures effectively.

One theory of learning to gesture is that you should simply "be natural" and allow the gestures to occur spontaneously. But this advice is incomplete. Most of us have acquired a few poor habits of posture or a few distracting mannerisms of bodily movement. Such bad habits should be spotted by practicing in front of a large mirror and by securing advice from your instructor. You should then experiment to find the new way of standing or walking or gesturing which *looks* natural and, having found it, you should practice until the new way becomes habitual. Then the advice to "be natural" will become superfluous; the habitual way is the natural way.

You should also consider the close relationship between habits and spontaneity in bodily action. You can practice various common gestures alone or in this class until the ways by which you make those gestures become habitual. Then in giving a talk you can concentrate your attention entirely upon your ideas and your audience; when the impulse to gesture occurs, you will gesture automatically. Furthermore, the habits you have previously formed will now assure that the gesture is effectively made, and that it will not be incomplete, or an awkward sawing of the air. Thus mechanical habits eventually become an integral part of spontaneity.

INSTRUCTIONS

You have doubtless heard the ancient challenge to describe a spiral staircase, using only words; you have found that an effective description requires that at least half of the communication be bodily and the other half verbal. In this assignment you will undertake a similar challenge. About half the communication will be bodily and half verbal. Mix together the visual and the auditory elements so that they combine into an integrated whole.

Much will depend upon your choice of a topic. Select a subject of personal knowledge and interest to you, one that requires considerable bodily action. Some themes obviously demand only minute movement while others necessitate broad action. Choose

77

the latter. Practice, if possible, before a large mirror. When you use a gesture, *carry it through.* Do not be timid and half-hearted but use all bodily action boldly and wholeheartedly.

Do *not* use visual aids; in a sense you will be your own best visual aid.

SUGGESTED TOPICS

How to do a given dance step
On being attacked by bees
Movie stuntmen's tricks
How to play tennis or table tennis
Various swimming strokes
Modeling clothes
Dribbling and shooting in basketball
Body-building exercises
The most awkward man I've known

Fencing
Different ways of walking
Cheerleaders' routines
Orchestra conducting
Measuring the size of this room
Shadowboxing
A football referee's signals
Military marching

18

pantomimes

OBJECTIVE

Ordinary speech communication is a combination of visual and auditory stimuli. Silent motion pictures illustrate the use of the visual stimuli alone; radio broadcasts illustrate the auditory alone. The purpose of this project is to study the possibilities and the limitations of nonverbal communication through visual stimuli alone.

BACKGROUND

The history of pantomime would make a good topic for a talk later in this term. Its origin may be traced back to primitive cultures. In ancient Rome elaborate pantomimes, commonly portraying well-known myths, were enacted by masked players. Beginning about the sixteenth century, pantomime developed such traditional characterizations as Harlequin, Columbine, and Scaramouch. More recently, pantomime achieved new dimensions through the work of Charlie Chaplin, Buster Keaton, and others of the silent film era. And today we have the unforgettable artistry of the great French pantomimist, Marcel Marceau.

The tools of pantomime include physical appearance, dress, posture, walk, gesture, and facial expression. By means of these tools you can communicate many ideas without benefit of spoken or written words. In fact, there are some ideas that can be expressed better by visual signs than by any other means—a shrug, a smile, a nod can sometimes be more eloquent than any words. On the other hand you have probably had enough experience with the party game of charades to know that certain ideas are difficult or impossible to express without the use of arbitrary language symbols.

During the course of this project you should devote some independent thinking to these questions: What kinds of ideas are best suited to expression by visual means alone? What kinds are unsuited or impossible? To get your thinking started, consider the following example. You can express by actions alone, "These are the basic steps of the waltz." But can you similarly express, "All dance steps have something in common"?

INSTRUCTIONS

The class will be divided into teams of two or three. Each team will agree upon an idea to be presented as a brief pantomime; they will prepare and rehearse beforehand in accordance with the instructor's arrangements.

In practicing and presenting the pantomime strive for free uninhibited movement. Put yourself into the mood and spirit of the skit; be alert and responsive to the actions of the others; do your own part wholeheartedly. Try to avoid jerky uncompleted gestures and random, purposeless, distracting movements. Facial expression is especially important.

SUGGESTED TOPICS

Choose a situation or setting and invent a simple story or incident to go with it. Each team should endeavor to think of something original and ingenious. The following suggestions are intended to indicate the type of setting and plot that you are likely to find useful:

Swimming pool or beach. A swimmer in distress is rescued and given artificial respiration.

High school dance. Bashful (or aggressive) boy asks timid (or sophisticated) girl for the next dance.

Restaurant. A busy waiter meets two indecisive customers.

Baseball game. The eternal battles between the pitcher, the batter, and umpire.

Busy intersection. When one car bumps the car ahead while stopping for the signal, the irate drivers and the traffic cop talk things over.

Used car lot. The salesman struggles to find a car that will please both the husband and the wife.

Orchestra rehearsal. The conductor has his troubles with a violinist and the kettledrummer.

Courtroom. The defendant and his lawyer are eager to impress jury members with good will, integrity, and innocence.

Reducing salon, People will undertake some remarkable contortions for the sake of a good figure.

19

visual aids

OBJECTIVE

Can you explain how to tie a bowknot without using a shoelace, piece of cord, or a similar visual aid? Try it—using words alone—and you will find that explaining this simple operation becomes a nightmare of complexity.

The purpose of this assignment is (1) to give you personal practice in supporting a point by the effective use of visual aids of your own choice, and (2) to provide an opportunity to observe a variety of types of visuals.

BACKGROUND

Experimental research, especially in the field of instructional technology, has indicated that the addition of visual aids to a talk usually produces three valuable results: (1) increased audience attention, (2) increased initial understanding, and (3) longer retention of the speaker's ideas. Educational TV programs for children are especially vivid examples of the virtues of nonverbal visuals. But on a more complex level the values of visual aids apply equally to adults. Our own experience confirms these findings. "Look, it works this way," are words that preface much of our learning.

Using the classroom chalkboard is such a familiar ritual in student experience that it should be avoided during this assignment; be more inventive and ingenious. Consult someone knowledgeable about local audio-visual equipment and services (new gimmicks are being invented all the time). Perhaps you can arrange to use an overhead projector, VTR (video

tape recorder), slides, transparencies with overlays, film strips, or portable TV receiver. Especially interesting might be a homemade visual of your own, for example, something made with posterboard and paints. Do not give a commonplace talk illustrated by a commonplace object, such as how to grip a golf club. However, the possibilities of a common object used in an uncommon way might stimulate your imaginative powers. Part of your responsibility in this project is to give your colleagues new ideas on visual aids.

This project will help your understanding of the close relationship between verbal and nonverbal communication. The mere display of an object is usually ambiguous or meaningless when not accompanied by spoken explanation. A chart or diagram with dates, quantities, or labels on it is a combination form—printed words are just as "verbal" as spoken ones.

INSTRUCTIONS

Your instructor may specify a brief talk in which you clarify a single point, or he may assign a longer talk with two or more main points. In either case the logic of a deductive sequence is recommended (review Project 7 and the sequence on page 22).

Choose your topic with special care; the development of your idea should either necessitate a visual aid or suggest that a visual aid is the best choice among the several forms of support. Thus the visual is integral to the talk—not something dragged in or tacked on.

Your choice of topic must be made simultaneously with your choice of visual aids. Your ideas about the latter may be stimulated by reviewing your textbook, other speech communication texts, and books on instructional technology. What you want is an up-to-date listing of the variety of potential visuals.

Major characteristics of effective visual aids include good visibility, simplicity, and dynamism.

Visible to entire audience. The visual aids should be large enough for group presentation. Sometimes small diagrams, objects, or pictures can be transferred to slides and projected on a portable screen. The display of visuals requires proper placement in terms of the audience and room layout. The lighting of the room may require advanced planning.

Simple enough to be understandable. Don't clutter the visual aid with nonessential details. Avoid cramming too much information into charts or diagrams. Perhaps the subject matter should be divided into steps or other logical parts, using a separate visual aid for each subdivision, showing them in some type of logical sequence.

Dynamic enough to sustain interest. A single chart showing, say, a typical sales curve for TV sets since 1945 may soon appear static and may become a distraction as the talk proceeds. One solution is to remove the chart as soon as the audience has had time to grasp the point. But it would be much better to rethink and redesign the visual aid. The goal would be to create an illusion of an ongoing event or process or series of happenings. Many improvements are possible. Perhaps the simplest way would be to reveal the chart in progressive segments by means of a second piece of posterboard, sliding it from left to right as the talk progresses. Or the segments could be presented in sequence by use of a set of flip-charts. The significance of the TV sales curve might be enhanced by including adjusted growth curves for radio sets, movies, and newspapers—the additional curves might

well be in different colors. A more sophisticated and flexible procedure for accomplishing any of the above suggestions would be the use of transparencies with overlays. Any of the suggestions would help to produce an illusion of a dynamic process which grows or evolves during the speech, reaching the completed picture near the end of your talk. A variety of other ingenious techniques have been developed in recent years which can add to the effectiveness of visual aids. And of course some objects or models provide actual movement rather than the illusion of it. You can allow the audience to see a visual "grow" (but only if you have the necessary talent and skill) by drawing a cartoon, sculpting a figure, or assembling a mechanical tool. Practice beforehand, keeping in mind the following suggestions:

1. Do not block the audience's view—stand to one side of the visual aid.
2. Point to specific parts of the visual aid when appropriate; use a pointer; and use the hand and arm nearer to the visual aid.
3. Avoid surplus distracting movements; do not handle the visual aid except as required for demonstration purposes.
4. Talk to the audience, not to the visual aid.
5. You may use notes, but do not rely upon them too heavily. You will find that visual aids themselves become a set of notes, reminding you of your planned ideas.
6. Study the Criticism Chart, pages 83–84.

SUGGESTED TOPICS

Anatomy of the eyes
Marriage and divorce rates
The art of theatrical or other make-up
Trends in women's (or men's) fashions
Freeway (or other transportation) networks
The population explosion
Optical illusions
How to read blueprints
Urban planning
How a communications satellite works

Our gross national product (GNP)
How to use home electrical tools
Public opinion polling
Color mixtures and combinations
Federal financing of education
The speech and hearing mechanisms
The problems of air pollution
Human communication models
Our national defense (strategies and/or budgets)

NAME_____ TIME _____ TO_____ TOTAL _____

TOPIC_____ VISUAL AIDS _____

<u>Speech content and structure</u> 1 2 3 4 5

   Opening 1 2 3 4 5

      Aroused favorable attention:

      Gave preview:

      Aroused "a need to know":

   Body 1 2 3 4 5

      Choice of points:

      Sequence of points:

      Development of each point:

   Conclusion 1 2 3 4 5

      Summary or perspective:

      Concluding words:

<u>Effectiveness of visual aids</u> 1 2 3 4 5

   Visibility 1 2 3 4 5

      Too large, about right, too small

      Clear view, speaker blocks view, other interferences

      Well located, too far back, too near, poor angle

Simplicity and clarity   1   2   3   4   5

> Understandable on sight: yes, no, doubtful

> Immediate impressions of the visual: clear, interesting, too many details, oversimplified, poorly constructed, eye-catching, too commonplace, instructive, confusing, did not "say" much

> Initial explanation: needed, not needed, too lengthy, too brief, too involved, too technical, well done, outstanding

Dynamic qualities   1   2   3   4   5

> An integral part of talk, partially so, "tacked on"

> Useful only once, several times, all of the time

> Usefulness grew, became static, became distracting

> Imaginative, ingenious, novel, bizarre

> Caught attention, helped sustain interest, failed to interest

Handling of visual aids   1   2   3   4   5

> Initial presentation: properly timed, too soon, too delayed

> Referring or demonstrating: well done, too little, too much

> Physical movement: too much, about right, not enough

> Handling or pointing: skillful, awkward, acceptable

> Directness: talked to audience, talked to visual aid, kept looking at _____

20

"the silent strangers"

OBJECTIVE

This project sets up an intriguing encounter between you and two strangers. They will visit the class for 15 or 20 minutes but will not utter a word. You will have ample opportunity to watch them, and you will be challenged to deduce as much information as you can, judging from nonverbal (mostly visual) cues only.

BACKGROUND

Some people cultivate the hobby of systematically observing strangers while riding on a bus or plane, waiting in a reception room, or attending social gatherings; then they make conclusions about the personalities of these "subjects." Most of us do not make a hobby of this Sherlock Holmesian game, yet on occasion we do try to size up another person by deliberately evaluating his appearance and body movements; and most of us regularly try to make a favorable impression on others by improving our appearance, through hair styling, selecting clothes, dieting, sun tanning, using cosmetics, and so on. Social scientists for many years have been testing the general hypothesis that people are constantly communicating with one another, consciously or subconsciously, by nonverbal signs (interrupted occasionally by verbaliza-

tions). For example, the eminent communications researcher Ray Birdwhistell has published many articles and books devoted to the specialized area which he has called the science of *kinesics*.

The mere presence of an obvious stranger in a "closed" group communicates something, sometimes mostly questions. In this project the focus is upon one question, "What kind of person is this?" You must base your answer on nonverbal cues: general appearance and physique, posture, clothing, facial expression, walking and other everyday body movements, and perhaps visible mannerisms. How much can you tell for sure, and how accurately can you make educated guesses? You may well wonder if this living picture is indeed "worth ten thousand words."

INSTRUCTIONS

The date for the visit by the strangers will be announced in advance so that you will have time to read about this project and study the inventory items which may suggest ways of sharpening your observations. Meanwhile, the instructor will arrange outside of class for the appearance of the strangers (perhaps one of each sex). The instructor may tell them to behave naturally or to play a role. The strangers will enter at the beginning of the meeting or during it; they should be seated so that the class has a good view of them, especially their faces.

The instructor will then lead a class discussion of nonverbal communication; relevant references to the

strangers may be made, although of course such references should not be overdone. After about 15 minutes, the instructor will thank the visitors and they will silently leave the room.

The instructor may ask the class to discuss the episode immediately, using the Inventory, pages 87–90, as a discussion guide. If the instructor wants a deeper coverage, the members of the class may first fill out the inventory independently and then the resulting data may be used as a discussion guide.

You will note in general that although the strangers speak no words, their behaviors "say something."

NAME_____ DATE _____

I. Reactions to the event itself

   A. Before the strangers arrived, my attitude was mostly:

      (curiosity, anticipation, disinterest, etc.)

   B. When I first saw the strangers as they entered, I felt:

      (surprised, disappointed, uneasy, etc.)

   C. During the ensuing discussion period, I felt:

      (stimulated, antagonistic, bored, etc.)

   D. When the strangers departed, I felt:

      (relieved, appreciative, apathetic, etc.)

   E. In general:

      1. I was more favorably impressed by stranger X (than Y).

      2. I was more favorably impressed by Y (than X).

      3. I liked both of them.

      4. I disliked both of them.

      5. I had practically no reaction to either of them.

II. Reactions to stranger X

    A. Factual judgments (can be verified):

        1. X's age, weight, height

        2. X is a student here, is from another school, is not a student

        3. Role playing or being natural

        4. Nervous or at ease

        5. Has had speaking or acting training

        Other:

    B. Value judgments (matters of opinion):

        1. X is aggressive, submissive

        2. Extrovertive, introvertive

        3. Good looking, homely, ordinary

        4. Upper class, middle class, lower class

        5. Friendly, unfriendly

        6. Well dressed, inappropriately dressed, sloppy

        Other:

    C. Personal conclusions:

        1. I would like to know X better

        2. I would *not* like to know X better

        Other:

III. Reactions to stranger Y

    A. Factual judgments (can be verified):

        1. Y's age, weight, height

        2. Y is a student here, is from another school, is not a student

        3. Role playing or being natural

        4. Nervous or at ease

        5. Has had speaking or acting training

        Other:

    B. Value judgments (matters of opinion):

        1. Y is aggressive, submissive

        2. Extrovertive, introvertive

        3. Good looking, homely, ordinary

        4. Upper class, middle class, lower class

        5. Friendly, unfriendly

        6. Well dressed, inappropriately dressed, sloppy

        Other:

    C. Personal conclusions:

        1. I would like to know Y better

        2. I would *not* like to know Y better

        Other:

IV. Overall Evaluation of the Event

Write below a brief essay on this project as a concrete example of the broad topic of non-verbal communication:

21

voice recordings

OBJECTIVE

If you have never before heard a recording of your own voice, you are due for a surprise. If you have heard recordings of your voice, you probably did not pay much attention to details; you may have thought of the recorder as a toy rather than as a tool. This assignment will introduce you to the value of recordings as a technique in analyzing, evaluating, and practicing to improve your own speaking voice, especially through self-criticism.

You have undoubtedly heard recordings of well-known contemporary public speakers and readers, but again you probably made no systematic study of the vocal techniques you were hearing. A second objective of this assignment will be to show you how you can improve your own vocal communication by analyzing recordings of other speakers.

BACKGROUND

When you listen to someone talking, you should distinguish between the verbal and the vocal components; the vocal is the nonverbal. If you say with a downward inflection, "You take the blame," that expresses an opinion or a command. If you say the same words with a rising inflection, the meaning is transformed into a question, "You take the blame?" In either case the meaning can be further altered by changing your vocal stress from one word to another. In the present project we will focus on the vocal or nonverbal component of your talking. The most efficient way to study this involves the use of voice recording equipment.

There are many types of audio recording equipment but we shall confine our discussion to tape recordings and phonograph records. These two are the most commonly used and most widely useful in the training of beginning students of speech. Many students can afford to buy a cassette recorder; there are several inexpensive yet adequate models. Any student can afford to buy at least one good album of speeches, readings, or plays; dozens have been produced by all major record companies.

When you begin to listen critically to the voice of a speaker, in person or by recordings, you have begun what is called "ear training." You are training yourself to listen for and to hear vocal details to which you have not formerly paid attention. To get started on this, we should immediately set up some stand-

ards. There are four major characteristics of an acceptable speaking voice. It is (1) audible, (2) distinct and accurate, (3) meaningful, and (4) pleasant.

Audibility. The audience should be able to hear all the words without straining. One common fault is illustrated by the student who begins each sentence bravely, then gradually runs down, allowing the ending to trail away into complete inaudibility.

Distinctness and accuracy. The speaker is required to articulate all sounds properly and pronounce his words according to an acceptable standard. Many faults are common on campus: slurring, sound substitutions, sound omissions, mispronunciation of ordinary words. All four of these faults are illustrated when a student says something like,"Jist whirl at git-cha?" ("Just where will that get you?")

Meaningfulness. Subject matter, logic, language, and bodily action are some of the factors that contribute to meaningfulness, but one of the most important is the proper use of vocal variety. Lack of vocal variety—monotony—is the criticism most often deserved by beginning speakers. There are four major aspects of the speaking voice where meaningful variety should be achieved; these are (1) rate, (2) loudness, (3) pitch, and (4) quality. Some students lack all four kinds of variety; other students may have achieved one kind but not another; still others may use variety but in such fashion as to be meaningless or misleading.

Pleasantness. The individual quality of a voice

should produce a favorable impression upon listeners. Pleasant vocal qualities may be described as resonant, mellow, vibrant, musical; unpleasant qualities as strident, harsh, nasal, breathy.

The above standards will provide you with a frame of reference which will help you to describe and evaluate a speaking voice—somebody else's or your own. To make your analyses more systematic, voice criticism charts are provided on pages 93–100.

After you have made a thorough analysis of your own voice the next step is to plan a program for improvement. Let us say, for instance, that you need to improve your vocal variety. At this point you need to realize what the possibilities are, what *can* be done. Here is where phonograph records of successful speakers and actors should be used. Analyze the vocal variety of such speakers as Winston Churchill, Agnes Moorehead, Laurence Olivier, Judith Anderson, Raymond Massey, Richard Burton. Vocal variety will soon acquire new dimensions.

INSTRUCTIONS

1. Your instructor may wish to use one class meeting to familiarize you with recording equipment, and to let you hear a brief sample of your own voice in direct comparison with the voices of the other students. The class may be divided into pairs. Each pair decides upon a topic, such as the most recent football game, and gets its turn to sit at the microphone and converse impromptu for one or two minutes. The tape may be played back immediately after all have spoken; the instructor may stop the machine from time to time, calling attention to good and bad examples of various aspects of voice.

2. For first practice in using the criticism charts, the instructor may play for the class a recording by an unknown student from some other class. You will listen carefully and fill out one of the charts. The instructor may then see how much you have heard and how well you judged. He may call attention to a good many things that you failed to hear.

3. The class may be divided into pairs who will meet outside of class. With or without the aid of a recorder, each student prepares a criticism chart on his colleague's voice. This gives you another chance to practice using the chart, and also gives you some insight into how you sound to other people.

4. The most important part of this project is for you to do a thorough critique of your own voice. Here you will need to make a tape recording. Suggestions for materials to be recorded: give a portion of a speech you recently gave in class; read a brief excerpt from a speech printed in your textbook, recent newspaper, or the like; just converse with the mike about some personal experience. Play back this recording several times, making notes each time on a few aspects of the voice. The final draft of your critique should be typed or neatly written in ink.

5. Obtain a phonograph record of a favorite speaker, reader, or actor. Play it several times, making notes on all aspects of voice and articulation. Using these notes, prepare one of the criticism charts. Obviously this critique will be slanted differently from your previous ones. Here you are not proposing a program for the speaker's improvement; you are looking for good examples of vocal techniques which will help you in setting goals for your own improvement. So most of the details on the chart should be reported "in reverse"; that is, describe how the speaker avoided the common mistakes. Perhaps you will add a type-written page of specific examples of vocal skill which you find helpful.

ANALYSIS OF _____ DATE_____

ANALYZED BY _____

Rate   1   2   3   4   5

    Too fast:

    Too slow:

    Unvarying; monotonous:

    Poor phrasing (choppy or jerky):

    Hesitations; vocalized pauses ("and-uh"):

Audibility   1   2   3   4   5

    Too loud:

    Too weak:

    Endings trail away:

    Muffled (mouth not open enough):

    Monotone or monotonous pattern of loudness:

    Force overused as a form of emphasis:

Pitch   1   2   3   4   5

    General level too high:

    General level too low:

    Lack of variety; monotony:

    Fixed pitch pattern monotonously repeated:

    Singsong; chanting; bedtime-story effect:

    Lack of relationship between pitch changes and meaning:

    Exaggerated pitch changes:

Quality (pleasantness, resonance)   1   2   3   4   5

Favorable descriptive words are:

Unfavorable: nasal (hillbilly twang), denasal ("cold in the head" voice), hoarse, breathy, throaty, guttural, strained, harsh, raucous, strident, flat, thin, falsetto, dull and lifeless, other

Articulation   1   2   3   4   5   And Pronunciation   1   2   3   4   5

Careless, lip-lazy:

Slurred, mumbled:

Too precise, affected:

Regional or foreign accent:

Sound substitutions:

Sound omissions:

Sound additions:

Specific defective sounds:

Pronunciation pedantic, nonstandard, dialectal:

Specific mispronounced words:

ANALYSIS OF_____ DATE_____

ANALYZED BY_____

Rate   1   2   3   4   5

Too fast:

Too slow:

Unvarying; monotonous:

Poor phrasing (choppy or jerky):

Hesitations; vocalized pauses ("and-uh"):

Audibility   1   2   3   4   5

Too loud:

Too weak:

Endings trail away:

Muffled (mouth not open enough):

Monotone or monotonous pattern of loudness:

Force overused as a form of emphasis:

Pitch   1   2   3   4   5

General level too high:

General level too low:

Lack of variety; monotony:

Fixed pitch pattern monotonously repeated:

Singsong; chanting; bedtime-story effect:

Lack of relationship between pitch changes and meaning:

Exaggerated pitch changes:

Quality (pleasantness, resonance)   1   2   3   4   5

Favorable descriptive words are:

Unfavorable: nasal (hillbilly twang), denasal ("cold in the head" voice), hoarse, breathy, throaty, guttural, strained, harsh, raucous, strident, flat, thin, falsetto, dull and lifeless, other

Articulation   1   2   3   4   5   And Pronunciation   1   2   3   4   5

Careless, lip-lazy:

Slurred, mumbled:

Too precise, affected:

Regional or foreign accent:

Sound substitutions:

Sound omissions:

Sound additions:

Specific defective sounds:

Pronunciation pedantic, nonstandard, dialectal:

Specific mispronounced words:

ANALYSIS OF _____ **DATE** _____

ANALYZED BY _____

Rate   1   2   3   4   5

   Too fast:

   Too slow:

   Unvarying; monotonous:

   Poor phrasing (choppy or jerky):

   Hestitations; vocalized pauses ("and-uh"):

Audibility   1   2   3   4   5

   Too loud:

   Too weak:

   Endings trail away:

   Muffled (mouth not open enough):

   Monotone or monotonous pattern of loudness:

   Force overused as a form of emphasis:

Pitch   1   2   3   4   5

   General level too high:

   General level too low:

   Lack of variety; monotony:

   Fixed pitch pattern monotonously repeated:

   Singsong; chanting; bedtime-story effect:

   Lack of relationship between pitch changes and meaning:

   Exaggerated pitch changes:

Quality (pleasantness, resonance)　　1　　2　　3　　4　　5

Favorable descriptive words are:

Unfavorable: nasal (hillbilly twang), denasal ("cold in the head" voice), hoarse, breathy, throaty, guttural, strained, harsh, raucous, strident, flat, thin, falsetto, dull and lifeless, other

Articulation　　1　　2　　3　　4　　5　　　　　And Pronunciation　　1　　2　　3　　4　　5

Careless, lip-lazy:

Slurred, mumbled:

Too precise, affected:

Regional or foreign accent:

Sound substitutions:

Sound omissions:

Sound additions:

Specific defective sounds:

Pronunciation pedantic, nonstandard, dialectal:

Specific mispronounced words:

21 **CRITICISM CHART**
ANALYSIS OF VOICE

ANALYSIS OF_____ DATE _____

ANALYZED BY_____

Rate   1   2   3   4   5

    Too fast:

    Too slow:

    Unvarying; monotonous:

    Poor phrasing (choppy or jerky):

    Hesitations; vocalized pauses ("and-uh"):

Audibility   1   2   3   4   5

    Too loud:

    Too weak:

    Endings trail away:

    Muffled (mouth not open enough):

    Monotone or monotonous pattern of loudness:

    Force overused as a form of emphasis:

Pitch   1   2   3   4   5

    General level too high:

    General level too low:

    Lack of variety; monotony:

    Fixed pitch pattern monotonously repeated:

    Singsong; chanting; bedtime-story effect:

    Lack of relationship between pitch changes and meaning:

    Exaggerated pitch changes:

Quality (pleasantness, resonance)   1   2   3   4   5

Favorable descriptive words are:

Unfavorable: nasal (hillbilly twang), denasal ("cold in the head" voice), hoarse, breathy, throaty, guttural, strained, harsh, raucous, strident, flat, thin, falsetto, dull and lifeless, other

Articulation   1   2   3   4   5   And Pronunciation   1   2   3   4   5

Careless, lip-lazy:

Slurred, mumbled:

Too precise, affected:

Regional or foreign accent:

Sound substitutions:

Sound omissions:

Sound additions:

Specific defective sounds:

Pronunciation pedantic, nonstandard, dialectal:

Specific mispronounced words:

22

content-free vocalization

OBJECTIVE

The purpose of this informal experiment is to acquaint you with the amounts and kinds of meaning that can be communicated by nonverbal vocal means.

What can you tell your listeners by tone of voice, pitch, loudness, and rate *alone*?

BACKGROUND

Legend has it that Sarah Bernhardt once moved her audience from laughter to tears during a solo performance in which the only words she used were numerals from a foreign language. Some of this *tour de force* would have depended upon visual stimuli; the rest of it would have depended upon her professional mastery of the vocal (nonverbal) stimuli. She could have isolated the visual by means of pantomime; in modern times she could have isolated the vocal by tape recorder or other electronic device.

Many intriguing research studies in recent years have explored the potentialities of what is commonly called "content-free" speech. Several methods have been used to achieve content-free speech, for example uttering only the numbers one-two-three-and so on in repetitious fashion, doing the same with letters of the alphabet or nonsense syllables, or recording an ordinary spoken message and then using electronic filter-

ing to make the words so unintelligible as to be meaningless. The researchers found that a surprising amount of meaning is a function of purely vocal characteristics of speech communication. You cannot convey information about a topic through vocal characteristics alone, but you can often reveal attitudes, emotions, and personal characteristics. Accuracy is another matter. Whether you can get across what you intend depends upon your vocal skill plus your listener's "ear."

Another line of speculation that should interest you is the influence of vocal characteristics alone at summit meetings or other international conferences requiring an interpreter. What is communicated by vocal sounds alone to and from the President of the United States and the Premier of the U. S. S. R. during a summit meeting? He's soft . . . He's tough . . . He's uncertain . . . and so on.

INSTRUCTIONS

Outside of class, make an audio recording, saying only the numerals one through ten in repetitious sequence (or if you prefer, use the first few letters of the alphabet). Divide the recording into the following three segments:

1. Try to show by voice alone the kind of person you think you are (or a role you are playing)—friendly, forceful, antagonistic, outgoing, introspective, and so on. (See Criticism Chart, page 103.)

2. Next, try to reveal your attitude towards your fictitious topic: favorable, unfavorable, and so on.
3. Finally, try to express several emotions (see some possibilities in the Criticism Chart). Make a list of the emotions in their sequence and bring it to class. While listening to your recording, your colleagues will make a list of the emotions they *thought* were conveyed. Then your list can be compared with those of the rest of the class to suggest how well you succeeded.

NAME _____ DATE _____

Instructions: The entire class will fill out this chart. Use either underscore or write-ins.

1. Personal characteristics suggested by the recording:

    Friendly, forceful, antagonistic, outgoing, introspective

    Other:

2. Attitude toward fictitious topic:

    a. Favorable   _____

    b. Unfavorable   _____

    c. Neutral   _____

    d. In a state of inner conflict _____

    e. Apathetic   _____

    f. Other   _____

3. Emotions that I thought were expressed during the recording:

    Anger, fear, happiness, sadness, merriment, sympathy, anxiety, love, sexual passion, hate, despair

    Other:

OTHER DIMENSIONS OF THE NONVERBAL

The visual and vocal stimuli discussed above are the most common and important nonverbal behaviors in ordinary speech communication, but you should not suppose that they are the only nonverbal dimensions. The scope of the entire subject can only be suggested here.

The effects of olfactory communication are pounded home by advertisements for a plethora of products: perfumes, deodorants for one's person or home or garbage pail, mouthwashes, shaving lotions, flowers, cooking spices, shampoos, and toothpastes. We communicate through the gustatory (taste) sense when we offer someone gifts of candy, tobacco, fruit, gum, or drinks; inviting people to dinner is an act of social communication.

The sense of touch may be the most basic of our communicative sensory modalities. All of us tend to rely on touching things as our best proof of reality when we suspect that our eyes or ears have deceived us. Various kinds of information about our environment require tactile experiences—the meanings of textures, edges, or dangerous sharp objects. The vital role of touching things is underscored by studies of communication among the blind. We all communicate through handshakes, embraces, kisses, pats or slaps or pokes or squeezes or pinches on shoulders, face, buttocks, and so on. You might reflect upon the contribution of tactile communication to the physical health and social development of infants; the newborn child and its mother communicate through mutual tactile experiences—nursing, caressing, cuddling, and patting. Sexual intercourse, necessary for procreation, normally involves the most intimate and massive tactual stimulation.

We have more than the traditional five senses. Equilibrium, pain, temperature, and kinesthetic sensations—all play important roles in communication with ourselves and others. The temperature of the classroom can influence the success of your talk for today. In his widely known book *The Silent Language*, Edward T. Hall has called attention to the importance of such nonverbal communication stimuli as territoriality and temporality. Thus standing too close or too far away may communicate more than words in a conversation; arriving late for an appointment or leaving someone to cool his heels in the outer office, may communicate disrespect or discourtesy or insult.

Being present or absent at a meeting is communicative. And silence when speech is expected is about as clear an example of nonverbal communication as can be imagined.

four

basic types of speech communication

If two cave dwellers wanted to do anything *together* and had no mode of intercommunication, they would have to invent one. Otherwise they could not even cooperate in removing a fallen tree from the trail. (One might wryly add that when a third caveman joined the group, politics was born.) When families, tribes, villages, and nations seek to carry on social and political life, they face some intrinsic problems—to pool information, to exchange thoughts and feelings, to choose group goals or policies, and to coordinate multi-individual actions. The need to survive forced primitive man to evolve ways of coping with these unavoidable problems. An inherent element in solving each problem was intercommunication. So basic types of speech communication evolved to match the basic types of social and political problems.

Thus it is not surprising that the rhetoricians of ancient Greece insightfully discussed the characteristics of speeches to inform, to convince, and to persuade—the accumulated experiences of centuries were already available. Nor is it surprising that the past twenty additional centuries have not produced radically new or different basic types of speech communication. However, modern rhetoricians and communication scientists have added refinements to speakers' strategies and have begun to probe into the crucial but almost invisible process of listening. So the projects in Section Four combine the old with the new—the traditional basics plus new scientific insights.

23

impromptu talk

OBJECTIVE

This project will provide practice in meeting those occasional emergency situations where you are unexpectedly called upon to "say a few words." You will undertake to apply rapidly some of the speech techniques that you have been studying, and you will taste the exhilarating experience of "thinking on your feet."

BACKGROUND

At a company sales conference, the department chief turns to you and says, "Ed, you've had experience with problems of this sort. What's your reaction?" While you might elect to mull over the question and take a day or two to organize your thoughts, this leisurely preparation period is not available. Twenty persons lean forward to hear your response—immediately! Men and women often are called upon at short notice to address groups. Usually, they talk about matters relating to their own specialty or about themes they are particularly equipped to discuss. Such talks, then, lack the specific detailed preparation associated with most speech making, but they do draw upon the broad preparation implicit in the speaker's career. Impromptu speech, in this sense, is not unprepared public speaking.

In the presentation of the impromptu talk, the speaker begins with three factors in his favor: (1) Customarily he is expected to speak on a theme with which he is familiar; (2) He usually is requested to speak on a specific topic and within a definite area; (3) Although time is limited, he does have a handful of moments in which to organize his thoughts and plan his comments.

Experienced speakers offer us helpful steps to succesful impromptu speaking. First, decide quickly upon one major idea or point to be advanced, phrasing this in the form of a direct statement. Second, try to think of an anecdote from personal experience that will support or illuminate the main point. At the same time look about the room to see if there is some object which might be woven into the talk as a visual aid. Third, find an opening that will capture immediate attention. Try to arouse curiosity and to create a desire to hear what is coming next. If possible, the first three steps should be accomplished in the minute or two before you begin to speak. Fourth, as you are speaking, think ahead to an effective way of closing—one that will imbed your major idea in the listeners' minds.

Audiences recognize the pressure under which the impromptu speaker is placed. They are, therefore, doubly appreciative of confidence and enthusiasm displayed by the speaker. Apologies are superfluous. Efforts at originality and humor, interesting asides, and imaginative organization find an unusually warm reception. To aid in fluency, frequent pauses are recommended. These seconds gained through pauses enable the speaker to decide upon his next words, and suggest self-assurance. If the speaker can forget himself, thinking only of conveying his idea, he will achieve audience impact.

INSTRUCTIONS

There are several interesting ways of setting up a round of impromptu practice speeches. Four choices are described below. Your instructor may wish to use one or more of these methods.

1. The instructor specifies a general topic to which all the impromptu speeches are to be related. Sample topics: preventing accidents, the power of positive thinking, the values of a college education. Then he

places a large sack or box on the desk; in it are a number of objects in common use, such as an eraser, safety pin, battery cell, key, or what have you. A student draws an object at random; he is given one minute in which to prepare mentally a one-minute talk pertaining to the announced topic and using the object as a visual aid to support his point. Just as the student is starting his talk, a second student draws an object from the box, so that each student prepares his talk during the one minute in which his predecessor is speaking.

2. The instructor prepares a set of file cards; on each card is a topic of general interest and knowledge. The first student draws a card from a container and is given one minute to think before beginning his talk. Just as in the previous assignment, a second student draws a card when the first student begins his remarks. Some sample topics:

Television commercials
Is woman's place in the home?
If I had it to do over again
The best speech I ever heard
My favorite airline
What I consider a good movie
What this school needs most
Generation gaps
City versus country living
The most useful profession
Should gambling be legalized?
Is honesty the best politics?
The ideal wife
Psychology

3. The instructor prepares a set of file cards; on each card is written a challenging quotation. The procedure for drawing the cards is the same as that described above. The student may either agree or disagree with the statement on the card. Some sample quotations:

"In politics one doesn't have friends, only allies."
—John F. Kennedy

"America is like a large friendly dog in a small room. Every time it wags its tail it knocks something over." —Arnold Toynbee

"Even when the experts all agree, they may well be mistaken." —Bertrand Russell

"Men always try to make virtues of their weaknesses." —H. L. Mencken

"American women expect to find in their husbands a perfection that English women only hope to find in their butlers." —Somerset Maugham

"An idea isn't responsible for the people who believe in it." —Don Marquis

"The fault, dear Brutus, is not in our stars, but in ourselves, that we are underlings." —William Shakespeare

"There is no good in arguing with the inevitable; the only argument available with an east wind is to put on your overcoat." —James Russell Lowell

"Half the modern drugs could well be thrown out the window, except that the birds might eat them." —Martin Fischer

"In America, the young are always ready to give to those who are older than themselves the full benefits of their inexperience." —Oscar Wilde

"You never really understand a person . . . until you climb into his skin and walk around in it." —Harper Lee

"The claim is that human existence is open-ended rather than predetermined, that it is characterized primarily by choice and contingency and chance rather than by compulsion." —Floyd Matson

"If we spend too much time debating the past, we may lose the future." —Edward R. Murrow

"This land was ours before we were the land's." —Robert Frost

"In the last analysis we are governed either through talk or through force." —Felix Frankfurter

"So leap with joy, be blithe and gay,
  Or weep, my friends, with sorrow.
What California is today,
  The rest will be tomorrow."
                    —Richard Armour

4. The instructor prepares a set of file cards; on each card is a question or problem pertaining to the materials which have been studied thus far in this class. Thus the assignment does double duty: it is a practice in impromptu speaking and also a test on course materials.

In any of the above four exercises, the procedure can be varied as follows: the student draws two objects or cards at random, quickly glances at them and makes a choice, keeping one and returning the other.

24

informative talk

OBJECTIVE

Lectures, reports, announcements, instructions, directions, book reviews, chalk talks, demonstrations—these are examples of occasions where the main job of the speaker is to present information. The purpose of this project is to give you an opportunity to practice several speech principles and techniques that are of special usefulness when you talk to inform.

BACKGROUND

The success of an informative talk must be judged by how much the audience understood and learned. It is not enough merely to present what you think are the most important facts about a subject; you must present them in such a way as to help the audience to grasp and remember those facts. Following are five suggestions for helping an audience to understand and learn.

Audience attention. The built-in booby trap of informative speaking is dullness; how many college lectures have put you to sleep or to daydreaming? To keep an audience not only awake but alert and interested, the speaker must show by mood, manner, and voice that he himself is interested. He should sprinkle the talk with attention-getting words, phrases, and sentences, for example, "The soil lost annually by erosion in the United States if loaded into boxcars would make a train stretching twice around the world." He should choose his materials with the interests of his specific future audience constantly in mind. And an occasional humorous anecdote or light touch has revived listeners at many business meetings, military briefings, and convention programs.

Audience motivation. When you begin preparing an informative talk, ask yourself, "Why should this particular audience want to receive this information?" Occasionally, you may feel that your topic is so vital to them that its mere mention will suffice to make them sit up and eagerly await your report. Usually your task is harder—they have to be told or shown. Therefore, early in the talk you must somehow stimulate the listeners' wish to be informed. Here are three common possibilities: (1) arouse their curiosity; (2) state or imply how they will benefit from knowing this information; (3) state or imply how they will be penalized by not knowing it.

Presentation of the unknown in terms of the known. Audience understanding is promoted by connecting your information with information familiar to the listeners. New facts are given meaning in terms of the facts we already know. For example, the problems of a motor pool supervisor become more understandable if he relates his occupational headaches to the difficulties of your own automobile. Translate the unfamiliar into everyday terms frequently in an informative speech.

Demonstration. Sometimes it is almost impossible to explain an object or a process by means of spoken words alone. To present a new first-aid technique effectively might require you to show exactly how it is done while you are talking about it. To clarify a point about choric speaking might require that you organize your audience into a verse-speaking choir and have *them* demonstrate your point by their own participation. To explain a mathematical formula might require that you work it out on a chalkboard as you talk.

Meaningful patterns of ideas. In planning the body of an informative talk, think back over the process by which you first understood and learned the information you are about to present. You will probably find that there were a few key points in your own learning process. You will probably find that at some stage all the points, parts, steps, or ideas rather suddenly clicked into position—and made a meaningful pattern.

Your job in this talk is to help the listener to learn better and faster than you did. So choose and word your main points with that learning process in mind. Then give a preview of these points early in the talk. Enumeration is often useful: "There are four main steps in this process." As you move from point to point, make the transitions unmistakably clear: "We now come to the second main step." You may need to summarize from time to time as you develop the body of the talk; almost certainly you will need to summarize at the conclusion.

INSTRUCTIONS

1. Class members may select any subject on which they wish to inform the audience. The topic should be one on which the speaker has personal experience or has gained special knowledge and one that serves a clarifying function for listeners. The subject should be delimited thoughtfully in order to meet the time limit, usually 6 to 8 minutes. Outlines may be recorded on the form provided on page 113, remembering the suggestions given in Project 9. Early in your preparation, carefully study the Criticism Chart on pages 115-16.

2. A variation of this assignment calls for attention to special types of informative talks. The instructor and class might decide to emphasize a particular form of informative talk, such as one of the following:

a. **Fact-finding report**. Assume that you have been asked by an organization to collect, condense, and evaluate information for them. Prepare an oral report appropriate for the hypothetical audience. Adjust to the time limits, record your outline, and study the Criticism Chart (see Instruction 1, above). Some additional suggestions:

(1) In your opening words reveal to the class the role it is to play; for example: "Mr. Chairman, Members of the Board of Education of Olney County— Six months ago you appointed a committee to make a survey of the teaching of reading in the elementary schools of this county. As chairman of that committee I will undertake to report our findings and recommendations."

(2) Identify the sources of your information: reading, correspondence, interviews, direct observations, etc.

(3) Interpret the information for your listeners: meanings, values, implications, or applications of the data.

b. **Book review**. Choose for review a current work of fiction or nonfiction from your major field of study. Select one on which you feel well qualified to report and which might profitably be read by other class members. As described above, adjust to your time limits, record your outline, and study the Criticism Chart. Limit your central idea by focusing on a theme or aspect of the book: Its timeliness, its significance, its provocative subject matter, its insight into your major field, its unique style, and so on. In selecting supporting materials consider the following:

(1) Critical comment from book reviews of the *New York Times, Saturday Review, Harper's,* the *Atlantic,* etc.

(2) The author and his background.

(3) Nature of content and points of highest interest. Read aloud any unusually interesting or distinctive passages for illustrative purposes.

(4) Evaluate the book as a whole. What was the author's purpose? Was it a worthwhile purpose? Did the author achieve his purpose?

c. **Historical narrative**. Select a period or sequence of events in history about which you feel qualified to speak. Study the Criticism Chart, adjust to time limits, and record the outline. In preparing your outline you may decide that you should simply tell a good story, and so you should. However, your goal is to inform. The following suggestions will illustrate that the principles of learning discussed under Background, above, are adaptable to historical narratives:

(1) Decide upon an appropriate place for a beginning.

(2) Determine key incidents that illustrate high spots of development or movement in the story.

(3) Indicate sources of information.

(4) When change occurs in the pattern or history being developed, offer reasons or causes for the change.

(5) Describe scenes, episodes, characters, and settings accurately and vividly.

SUGGESTED TOPICS

Modern techniques in dentistry
Psychedelic research

The sea as a food source
Traffic safety

The rise of Hitler
Jet engine development
Ideas of Jefferson
Works of C. P. Snow
Ten years of progress in electronics
Modern art
Cathedrals
The "roaring twenties"
Rehabilitation of the paraplegic

Solar energy
Systems of betting
Kabuki theater
The production of wine
Federal spending since 1960
The military briefing
Inside China today
Space exploration

24 OUTLINE FOR INFORMATIVE TALK

NAME_____ DATE_____

TOPIC_____

Type: Informal lecture   Fact-finding report   Book review   Historical narrative   Other

_____

Record your outline below; use the other side of this page if needed. Follow the suggestions and models in Project 9, pages 29–33.

Outline for informative talk, continued

25

persuasive speech

OBJECTIVE

This project has three objectives: (1) to provide practice in giving a speech that utilizes psychological principles of human motivation; (2) to provide practice in the use of a stock outline that is applicable to a wide variety of persuasive speeches; and (3) to improve your ability to evaluate persuasive appeals directed at you.

BACKGROUND

In a practical sense, the determination of whether a speech is informative or persuasive is made by the audience. The same speech may result in understanding and learning as well as in modification of attitudes; in fact, it is difficult to persuade without providing information, and *vice versa*. Nevertheless, it is useful to differentiate the two types of spoken communication in terms of the speaker's predominant aim: the goal of informative speaking is *clarification;* the goal of persuasive speaking is *influence.* The persuasive speech seeks to influence by building new beliefs, by strengthening existing ones, and by releasing beliefs into overt action.

We all know that persuasion may be used with equal facility by demagogues or democrats. Many of history's notable speeches are calls for belief and action in the name of fairness and justice, human dignity and freedom, social ideals and aspirations: Lincoln's quest for national unity, Churchill's denunciations of tyranny, Kennedy's call for renewal and commitment, and the appeal for brotherhood issued by Martin Luther King. On the other hand, persuasion may also be used by fanatics, racketeers, and swindlers who slant their misguided or bogus appeals at listeners who are often unwary. In defense of yourself and others, therefore, you should become familiar with persuasive techniques, including those that are most easily and often abused. A good place to begin your study is in front of the nearest television set. All advertisers, of course, are trying to sell their products; some do it ethically, others by unscrupulously tempting the audience with tantalizing (but often fallacious and sometimes dishonest) appeals to buy, try, and enjoy.

A good persuasive talk has logical as well as psychological validity. It is misleading to try to classify appeals as *either* intellectual *or* emotional; every appeal is a mixture of both; they are simply two aspects of the same thing. Suppose that we compare a speech to a loaf of bread. Every loaf of bread has both food value and flavor. The food value can be chemically tested in terms of calories, vitamins, minerals. The flavor can be evaluated by having one or more people taste it. A given loaf of bread may test high in food value but low in flavor, or vice versa, or high in both, or low in both. Similarly, every speech has both logical and psychological validity; the former can be tested in terms of the principles of evidence and reasoning; the latter in terms of audience motivation, belief, and action. A speech may rate high on one and low on the other, or low on both, or high on both.

Persuasion occurs when listeners perceive the speaker's message as so associated with their own motivations that they are willing to modify their individual attitudes in the direction desired by the speaker. The key terms are *associated* (or identified with) and *motivations*. Human motivations are numerous, complex, and interacting. However, the following four categories should provide a serviceable basis for the present project:

1. **Biological drives**: needs for food and shelter, comfort and security, physical health, and emotional well-being.
2. **Ego drives**: pride, dignity, self-respect; desires to create, to excel, to lead, to control, to achieve power.

3. **Social drives**: desires to "belong" and to win group approval, admiration, and status; family and community pride; patriotism, altruism.

4. **Habit drives**: desires to maintain customs, traditions, existing beliefs, existing intellectual and emotional patterns.

INSTRUCTIONS

1. Choose a sample of persuasion or propaganda, such as a political speech, an editorial, a printed advertisement, a pamphlet, a television commercial. Analyze it carefully in terms of its logical and psychological validity. Further details are included in the Analysis Sheet on pages 121–22.

2. Prepare a 5- to 7-minute persuasive speech for a specified audience. You may specify this class or a hypothetical audience, such as a student organization, a civic group, a labor union, a PTA, a business or professional club.

If most of the audience is already favorable to your proposal, your purpose will be to reinforce and strengthen their belief and probably to release that belief into overt action. If most of the audience is undecided about your proposal or hostile to it, your purpose will be to get them to make up their minds or change their minds—the final action sought will be belief with or without overt behaviors.

In preparing your speech you will use a stock outline which is especially useful for persuasive talks because it helps the speaker to combine sound logic and practical psychology into a single sequence. You plan the speech as a progression through four main steps:

a. **The attention step.** As in all speeches, your opening must get favorable attention and direct it to your subject.

b. **The need step.** The best way to get your listeners to believe or to act is first to get them to *want* to do it. You must arouse in them a feeling of need. Logically you say, "Something should be done for the following reasons." Successful persuasion requires that each "reason" be legitimately identified with an audience motive.

c. **The satisfaction step.** If your speech had been completely successful up to this point but then you suddenly sat down, the audience would feel disappointed and frustrated—they would have an urge to do something but you didn't tell them specifically what. Now you must tell them what you think they should believe or do. Logically you say, "I have a good proposal and I can prove it." But psychologically you describe your proposal to show how it will satisfy the needs or wants which have already been aroused—you let the listeners prove it to themselves. You can arouse a process of thought and feeling in a listener, but only he can complete it.

d. **The action step.** In your speech conclusion, you can help each listener by making perfectly clear just what he is expected to do—and when, how, where.

Make an outline of your talk, using the four-step design described above. Record your outline on the form on page 123. During the presentation of your speech your instructor may wish to utilize the Criticism Chart, pages 125–26.

SUGGESTED TOPICS

A talk in support of Community Chest
A speech on women's rights
A speech to a college audience on the dangers of smoking and drinking
A pro-margarine talk to dairymen
A reenlistment speech
A talk urging liberalized abortion laws
A speech on nationalized medicine to an AMA group

An address on urban renewal
A send-off talk to a Rose Bowl football team
Remarks by a fashion expert to a men's group
A desegregation speech to a Southern audience
A speech favoring (or opposing) the death penalty
A political speech to any audience
A talk by a warden to a group of rioting prisoners

CAMPAIGN PERSUASION

The purpose of campaign communication, says Stephen Shadegg, is "to address a persuasive request to every registered voter to support your candidate at the polls." We have frequent opportunity to observe the strategies and techniques of political persuasion. But how to assess them? The well-known communication model of Harold Lasswell can be adapted with the addition of feedback to the evaluation of campaign persuasion: *who* says *what*, through *what channels*, to *whom*, with *what effect*.

1. *Who*—the communicator, both as individual and as party representative.

    What is his personal and social background? Is he speaking for himself or for someone else?

    What has he said and done in the past? Is he consistent?

    Can you determine his outlook toward himself, others, and society? His world view?

    What is his personal stake in all this? Is it your stake? Are his goals in harmony with yours?

2. *What*—the message (content and presentation)

    What does it seem to say explicitly? Implicitly?

    What are the basic assumptions underlying the message? Can you infer the value-structure of the candidate?

    What verbal and nonverbal symbols were employed to reach the audience? Which were more persuasive?

    From what is communicated, can you judge the way in which the speaker (and his party) views the electorate?

3. *What channels*—the medium

    What reasons governed choice of the medium? Was it a good choice?

    Through what channels did the symbolic interaction occur?

    What effects did the setting have on speaker and audience?

    How did the medium influence or modify the message?

4. to *Whom*—the audience

    How was the audience organized? What interests were represented? Were any significant elements omitted?

    What conclusions could you draw about this audience: orientations, biases, motives, values, etc.?

    Could you gauge the level of listener interest or approval during the presentation?

    Why was this audience selected to receive the message?

5. *What effect*—the results

    What was the overt response to the message?

    How perceptively were the attitudes and predispositions of this audience estimated?

    Why was the desired response achieved (or not achieved)?

    How did the communication process contribute to the image of the candidate? (What are the dynamics of "image"?)

NAME _____ DATE _____

1. Brief description of the form and content of the sample analyzed:

2. Audience motives to which the persuader sought to appeal:

3. Description of one or more techniques used to touch upon audience motives (direct statement, indirect suggestions, slogans, pictures, name-calling, and so on):

4. Evaluation of the logical validity of the sample:

5. Evaluation of the psychological validity of the sample:

   a. Was it ethical?

   b. Did it persuade anyone? If so, who and why? If not, who and why not?

NAME _____ DATE _____

TOPIC _____

INTENDED AUDIENCE _____

1. The attention step:

2. The need step:

3. The satisfaction step:

4. The action step:

26

argument: direct

OBJECTIVE

This project has three objectives: (1) to provide practice in giving a speech that stresses the logical proof of a proposition; (2) to provide practice in the use of a stock outline applicable to a wide variety of argumentative speeches; and (3) to improve your ability to detect unsound reasoning and slipshod evidence. These objectives may be usefully compared with those for the preceding project.

BACKGROUND

In an argumentative speech you defend one side of a controversial question by means of logic and evidence; your purpose is to build or change beliefs and sometimes to release beliefs into overt action.

As was pointed out in Project 25, no speech can be 100 percent intellectual or 100 percent emotional; all speeches should be evaluated in terms of both logical and psychological validity. The difference between a persuasive and an argumentative speech is a difference in emphasis. Which emphasis to use should be decided in terms of the audience, occasion, and topic. Thus the argumentative speech may also be highly persuasive; certainly it should not reveal a neglect or ignorance of psychological principles of human motivation.

One important psychological principle affecting argumentative speaking is that frequently you are willing to reinforce the beliefs of your opponent(s) in order to influence the behavior of other listeners who are undecided. Thus political candidates do not really expect to win the votes already committed to each other; they argue against one another in order to sway undecided voters.

Each year more than 15,000 college and university students participate in intercollegiate debating while many thousands more take courses of intensive study in principles of argument. They recognize that skill in argumentative speaking is essential for business and professional life, in situations where judgments must be tested in the give-and-take of argument. The argumentative speaker seeks to influence the beliefs and behaviors of others by proving his points. Sometimes he must disprove or refute the arguments of an opponent. By *proof* we mean the content and structure of

evidence and reasoning which is intended to establish the probability that a given statement is true. *Refutation* refers to the process of undermining the proof, hence the argument, of an opponent.

Logical support of a proposition can be considered under two headings: evidence and reasoning. Evidence is the raw material of proof—facts and expert opinions. Sometimes facts are accepted because they are self-evident or because they are consistent with the audience's previous experience. At other times the reliability and validity of facts depend, as do opinions, upon the source or authority. The tests of evidence from a quoted source are as follows:

1. Is the source competent?
2. Is it biased?
3. Is that what was really said?
4. Is the evidence consistent?
5. Is the evidence documented or verifiable?

Reasoning is the process of drawing inferences or discerning relationships. Several common-sense tests are applied to the types of reasoning:

1. **Generalization** (reasoning from specific instances). Were enough examples presented? Were they typical instances? Were exceptions accounted for?
2. **Cause** (reasoning from phenomena and the means which produce them, or vice versa). Is there a connection between cause and effect? Is the cause sufficient to produce the alleged effect? Might other effects be produced by the cause in question?
3. **Analogy** (reasoning from comparison). Are the cases compared alike in essential respects? Do likenesses outweigh differences in the comparison?

INSTRUCTIONS

1. Find an example of a printed argumentative speech, editorial, commentary, or the like. Analyze the example in terms of main points, evidence, and reasoning as indicated on the form on pages 129–30.

2. Choose either the affirmative or negative side of a current controversial question. Read widely on both sides of the proposition and take notes on the evidence you find—facts, instances, statistics, and expert opinions. In preparing your outline adapt the main points and subpoints of the body of the outline from the stock design below. The four key words are *need, desirability, practicality,* and *alternatives.* This design implies a comparison between the affirmative side and the *status quo*—the existing system or attitude.

   I. Is there a need for a change?
      A. Are there existing or threatened evils?
      B. Are these evils due to the present system?
   II. Is the proposed change desirable?
      A. Will it eliminate or alleviate the evils?
      B. Will it provide additional advantages?
      C. Will it avoid new or greater evils?
  III. Is the proposal practical?
      A. Can it be satisfactorily financed and administered?
      B. Will it satisfy interest groups involved?
      C. Have similar systems succeeded in the past?
  IV. Is the proposal better than possible alternatives?
      A. Is it more desirable?
      B. Is it more practical?

Do not suppose that all of the above points and subpoints must be used in every argumentative speech. Sometimes it is sufficient to weigh the comparative advantages of alternative proposals. But think through each item and decide which ones are the most cogent and appropriate for your proposition, side, and audience. Then adapt your wording to suit the subject matter and audience motivation. You must also adapt to time limits of probably 8 minutes.

In the opening of the speech, state clearly the proposition and your position on it. Include also a preview of your main points. In the conclusion, summarize your arguments briefly; then in two or three hard-hitting sentences focus the whole speech on exactly what you expect the listeners to think, feel, or do.

In practicing and delivering the speech, be careful that in striving to be forceful you do not instead become dogmatic and belligerent.

SUGGESTED TOPICS

All college courses should be elective.

The United States should adopt compulsory national health insurance.

Modern advertising is detrimental to society.

Prayer should be restored to public schools.

Capital punishment should be abolished.

A moratorium should be declared on space exploration.

Labor union membership should not be a condition of employment.

Gambling should be legalized in America.

The sale of pornographic literature should be forbidden.

Foreign languages should be taught in elementary school.

The federal government should institute compulsory arbitration of labor disputes.

The United States should withdraw from the United Nations.

Student government in colleges is a failure.

A third major baseball league should be organized.

Intercollegiate football should be abandoned.

NAME _____ DATE _____

AUTHOR, TITLE, SOURCE OF EXAMPLE _____

_____

THE PROPOSITION TO BE PROVED WAS _____

_____

Main Points

    List them. Assuming that these points were true, would they suffice to prove the truth of the proposition? Why?

Evidence

What evidence, if any, was given to support each main point or subpoint? Was there sufficient evidence? Was the evidence valid and reliable?

Reasoning

What type or types of reasoning were used? Evaluate the reasoning.

NAME _____ **DATE** _____

PROPOSITION _____

_____

Introduction   1   2   3   4   5

Did the opening words get favorable attention?

Did speaker state his point of view early?

Did he give a preview of main points?

Was the transition into the body of the speech smooth?

Body   1   2   3   4   5

Was the central idea (proposition) clear?

Were the purpose and central idea sufficiently narrowed?

Did the main points suffice to prove the central idea?

Were there too many or too few main points?

Were the main points persuasively worded?

Was each main point supported by evidence?

Did the evidence include authorities, instances, statistics?

Was the reasoning from the evidence sound?

Was the speech adapted to audience interests?

Was the speech adapted to audience drives and motives?

Was the speech adapted to existing audience attitudes toward related topics?

Conclusion   1   2   3   4   5

Were the main points restated?

Did the conclusion focus the whole speech on the central idea?

Delivery   1   2   3   4   5

Visual:

Vocal:

Verbal:

General impressions:

27

argument: indirect

OBJECTIVE

In direct argument you begin by stating your chosen solution for a controversial problem and proceed directly to prove that your proposal should be accepted by the audience. In the present project, indirect argument, you begin by analyzing a controversial problem and show how you evolved a recommended solution. As in the preceding project, you will practice the use of solid evidence and sound reasoning. However, this time you will practice the use of a different type of speech design: the problem-solution sequence.

BACKGROUND

When should your argument be indirect rather than direct? One answer is that the problem-solution sequence is usually more effective during the earlier stages in the evolution of a public controversy. Controversial problems begin when something happens that makes people feel uneasy; they try to figure out what is the matter; a variety of possible solutions are proposed; most of these proposals are sooner or later rejected. Finally, only one or two proposals are left, and the time has come for making a decision. Indirect argument traces audience thinking through these evolutionary stages, and seeks to move that thinking forward toward making a reasoned decision.

During recent years substantial experimental research has compared the relative merits of one-sided versus two-sided argument. Roughly, the former is what we have called direct argument; and the latter, indirect. The experimental one-sided speeches present only arguments favoring a proposal; the two-sided speeches present both pro and con arguments. As you might suspect, the researchers have not found that either presentation is a panacea. However, support is given to the recommendation that in many situations the indirect argument is to be preferred. It is well adapted to the thoughtful but undecided listener, and the presentation of counterarguments in weakened form helps "inoculate" timid supporters against the danger of subsequently succumbing to an opposition speaker.

The indirect argument also eases the task of establishing early in the speech a sense of mutual identification between speaker and listener; the desired effect is "let's you and I think this through together." Then the speaker undertakes to carry the listeners step by step through his own process of investigation and thinking, and if he is successful the listeners will arrive at the same conclusion.

Much of what was written about the persuasive speech and direct argument is helpful in understanding the use of indirect argument. Therefore, you should review Projects 25 and 26. You will find that these three assignments should be viewed as a three-way partnership.

INSTRUCTIONS

Choose an appropriate topic and narrow it. You may choose a problem on which you either have or have not finally made up your mind. Use the stock design below to guide your research and thinking—it should prevent your overlooking a major logical question. Use the same design in making your speech outline, but you probably will not need to include all of the suggested points; for example, perhaps you know that practically the entire class already agrees that the problem is a serious one.

  I. Analysis of problem
  A. Is there a serious problem?
  B. Is it an inherent problem?
  C. What are its causes?
  D. What are the obstacles to its solution?

II. Finding a solution
    A. What are possible solutions?
    B. What standards should a good proposal meet?
    C. How do these several proposals compare in terms of your standards or criteria?
    D. What should be the final choice?

SUGGESTED TOPICS

Marriage and divorce
Freedom of the press
Gun control laws
Apathy in United Stated politics
Heroin and other hard drugs
Welfare programs
Crime on the streets
Labor-management relations

Ethnic studies programs
Race or religious prejudice
Foreign trade policy
Wiretapping
Prison reform
Agricultural policy
Rapid transit systems

Study the Criticism Chart on pages 135–36. Your instructor may wish to assign a written critique of a published speech in which indirect argument was used (or should have been used). If so, the Criticism Chart may furnish the guidelines for the written report. Therefore, two copies are provided.

NAME _____ DATE _____

TOPIC _____

Introduction   1   2   3   4   5

Did opening words get favorable attention?

Did he give a preview?

In his preview (and elsewhere in the introduction), did he tactfully avoid revealing his eventual solution?

Was transition into body of speech smooth?

Body   1   2   3   4   5

Did he begin with analysis of problem?

Did he begin on common ground, that is, aspects of the problem on which almost everybody would agree?

While analyzing the problem did he avoid leaping ahead to solutions?

Was his analysis clear?

Was it apparently unbiased?

Was the progression logical?

Was it convincing?

Was the transition into solutions satisfactory?

Did he discuss two or more solutions?

Was his discussion clear?

Was it apparently unbiased?

Was his choice of recommended solution logical?

Was it convincing?

Conclusion   1   2   3   4   5

Did he briefly summarize?

Did final words focus on exactly what he wanted audience to think, feel, or do?

Delivery   1   2   3   4   5

Visual:

Vocal:

Verbal:

General Impressions:

NAME _____ DATE _____

TOPIC _____

Introduction   1   2   3   4   5

Did opening words get favorable attention?

Did he give a preview?

In his preview (and elsewhere in the introduction) did he tactfully avoid revealing his eventual solution?

Was transition into body of speech smooth?

Body   1   2   3   4   5

Did he begin with analysis of problem?

Did he begin on common ground, that is, aspects of the problem on which almost everybody would agree?

While analyzing the problem did he avoid leaping ahead to solutions?

Was his analysis clear?

Was it apparently unbiased?

Was the progression logical?

Was it convincing?

Was the transition into solutions satisfactory?

Did he discuss two or more solutions?

Was his discussion clear?

Was it apparently unbiased?

Was his choice of recommended solution logical?

Was it convincing?

Conclusion   1   2   3   4   5

Did he briefly summarize?

Did final words focus on exactly what he wanted audience to think, feel, or do?

Delivery   1   2   3   4   5

Visual:

Vocal:

Verbal:

General Impressions:

28

communicative reading

OBJECTIVE

The minister quotes extensively from Scripture in his sermon, the political speaker concludes his campaign speech with a moving paragraph from Woodrow Wilson or Abraham Lincoln, the teacher of literature or philosophy laces his lecture with illustrative prose or poetry. Even the journeyman reporter, commentator, or debater makes unmistakably clear the importance of quoted percentages, figures, and trends. These speakers must be effective communicators of the written words of others. Indeed, with the time and censorship restrictions of modern platform, radio, and television speaking, an entire speech may be, in effect, a quotation of one's own words; that is, it requires skill in the communicative reading of a prepared manuscript which differs from the skill required for extemporaneous speaking.

The assignment in communicative reading offers (1) experience in the choice and use of extended quotations in the context of a speech, and (2) practice in basic techniques of reading aloud from the printed page.

BACKGROUND

Whether the words on the typewritten or printed page are your own or someone else's, the fact that they are embalmed in ink often destroys your communication of them. You are not using your own words spontaneously or at random; the thought processes and the language are fixed and sometimes strange. Too often, written materials are presented only in terms of their verbal message: the inexperienced reader pronounces, mumbles, or intones words without the physical and vocal dynamics which implement the intent of his speaking. Too often, the reading is mechanical or jerky or singsong, with head bent over the lectern and eyes glued to the manuscript. Another man's words must take the form of impressions, thoughts, and attitudes which you have made your own.

Good communicative reading has the following characteristics:

1. Quoted materials are relevant to the subject and purpose of the speech. Quoted materials are deliberately chosen to clarify, amplify, or prove a point. They are neither decoration nor diversion. If the point of the quote in the development of your speech is not instantly recognizable, you should make its relationship clear in comment.

2. Communicative reading is immediately comprehensible to the audience. Obviously, in order to read materials comprehensibly, you must comprehend them. You must understand (a) the theme and purpose of the materials, (b) the references and allusions, (c) the denotation and connotation of words, (d) the structure of ideas and attitudes in phrases, sentences, paragraphs, stanzas, and so on. This understanding will guide the vocal techniques of emphasis and subordination, inflection, grouping, pausing, tempo, and rate.

3. Communicative reading makes written materials more vivid to the listener than his own silent reading of them. Attitudes, emotional connotation of words, figurative language, sensory images, sound values, and rhythms are embodied in the reader's physical and vocal expression. These attributes of meaning and mood are best realized in reading aloud.

4. Communicative reading observes the principles of good platform deportment. The reader should be sufficiently familiar with his materials so that he is able to maintain eye contact with his audience as well as with the printed pages. This does not imply memorization; it does recommend analysis and oral practice with the manuscript. Gestures and movement are necessarily limited by use of the manuscript in hand or on the lectern. Generally, however, body movements may be used as in public speaking for reinforcement of meaning and attitude.

INSTRUCTIONS

Prepare a 6- to 8-minute talk in which quotations, read aloud from the printed page, are the major form of support. The quoted materials should make up 40 to 60 percent of the whole. Quotations should be drawn from more than one author, and from more than one type of material. Some types to consider: poetry, speeches, plays, essays, short stories, novels, general nonfiction, textbooks, technical reports. To avoid the temptation to talk in broad generalities and abstractions, you must word your central idea with special care. During your preparation, consult "Suggestions for Speaking from Manuscript," below.

SUGGESTED TOPICS

Voices of History
Political Campaign Slogans: The Quickie Appeal
The World of Ogden Nash
The Masculine Mystique
Yo soy Chicano
Revolt of the Consumer
Literature of Protest
The Jargon of Bureaucracy
I am Frightened by the "Brave New World"
Irish Eyes Aren't Smiling
To Be Black in America
What Is a University?
World War I Poets: The First Pacifists
Edward Albee's American Nightmare

SUGGESTIONS FOR SPEAKING FROM MANUSCRIPT

The reader-speaker should "think the thought at the moment of utterance." He must feel (and help the audience feel) that he is talking to and for them—in spite of the barrier of a script. The following techniques are used by successful manuscript speakers:

1. *Prepare manuscript carefully.* Have it typed in pica type, with fresh ribbon. Some speakers prefer upper-case letters throughout. Underline portions that deserve principal emphasis.
2. *Examine the script.* Pause before beginning. Take as long as you need to collect yourself and your thoughts. Control and poise are impressive and help consolidate audience attention.
3. *Look at your audience.* Recognize their presence. Don't open your eyes and mouth at the same time!
4. *Say the introduction* without looking at the script. The introduction may consist of a sentence, or several, or even a whole section. In any case, present as much as you can without losing contact with the audience.
5. When you look down, *keep your eye on the page until you come to a word, phrase, or part you want to emphasize*, then look up again. Repeated glances down and up are likely to confuse you and your listeners.
6. After looking up, *look at the audience until you are sure they have understood*. Don't hurry along. Look down while talking only when you want to suggest: "That which I am saying is not especially important; let me move to a more important part."
7. *Tell all examples or illustrations.* Material that doesn't demand exact wording is more effective if not read.
8. *Mark heavy (red) parentheses* around the portions that are to be given directly to the audience. Each person will vary in his markings depending upon amount of time for practice, confidence in ability to remember, and what he considers important.
9. If you forget what was written, or lose your place, *extemporize a new statement*. Since you are communicating ideas rather than words, be ready to change wording.

NAME _____ DATE _____

TOPIC _____

CENTRAL IDEA _____

The Quoted Materials   1   2   3   4   5

    Amount: about right, too little, too much

    Variety: excellent, satisfactory, too much from one source, too much same type

    Relevancy:

The Reader's Comprehension   1   2   3   4   5

    How well did the reader seem to understand the meaning of his chosen quotations?

Vocal Communication   1   2   3   4   5

    Audibility:

    Distinctness:

    Meaningfulness (phrasing, pause, inflection):

Visual Communication   1   2   3   4   5

    Directness:

    Facial Expression:

    Posture:

    Bodily movement:

29

listening exercise
for classroom use

OBJECTIVE

During this project the class will become a type of listening laboratory. The main objective is to provide listening practice with guidance. Guidance is given by means of (a) a listening chart with accompanying instructions, and (b) feedback from the speaker, instructor, and other class members.

BACKGROUND

We have earlier stressed the active role of the listener (pages 13–14). But the "continuing assignment" recommended was intentionally limited to a listener's reactions to selected aspects of a speaker's subject matter. Now let us go a step further.

A distinctive feature of a speech communication class is that you begin to form multiple-purpose listening habits. In other courses the instructor does most of the talking and you listen for the purpose of learning about his subject, either for its own sake or in order to make decent examination grades. In this course the students do most of the talking and you listen to them in order to find out (a) what the speaker has to say, (b) how he says it, and (c) whether you can profit from his example in your own future speaking. Thus you enlarge your listening repertoire.

In this project another variation of multiple-purpose listening will be put into practice. As you listen to an assigned student speaker, you will assume three roles: reporter, critic, and coach. The three functions are different yet closely interrelated. You will deliberately practice thinking of them "separately together." In doing the three things simultaneously, you may well expect to work much harder than the student who does the speaking.

A second value of this project is that you will serve as subject for one of your colleagues and receive his systematic analysis of the effects your speaking had on him, your hardest-working listener. He can help you to improve the accuracy of your self-image:

> O wad some Pow'r the giftie gie us
> To see oursels as others see us!
> It wad frae monie a blunder free us
> An foolish notion . . .
> —Robert Burns

INSTRUCTIONS

1. You will be assigned a student speaker on whom to practice listening. Now study the chart on pages 145–46. As listener, you notice that you are to provide three things: description, evaluation, and prescription; you are a reporter, critic, and coach. The speaker will notice that, at the bottom of the second page, he may talk back to you.

The largest amount of space is for description. Try to give a reasonably complete and objective report of what you saw and heard. Occasionally this may best be done by complete sentences (for example, his central idea), but key words and phrases (often quoted from the speaker) will usually suggest what ideas and behaviors impressed you the most as you listened. To guide your reporting, some familiar captions are supplied in the left-hand column. On the right-hand side is space for your evaluations, paralleling the items being criticized. You may use a grading system for some items, but usually your comments will be more instructive. For instance, suppose that under description you note "explains costs—$50,000 total"; under evaluation you might comment "too many confusing statistics" or "statistics clear and convincing." In general, evaluations should include both the favorable and unfavorable; it is almost inconceivable that any student talk would be either perfect or without a re-

deeming virtue. Some evaluative comments are sufficient unto themselves; others require suggestions on
how to improve (prescription). Thus, it is frustrating
to read only that the speech organization was "unclear" or "incohesive." Just what could the speaker
do about it? Perhaps you have a constructive suggestion: "Change from spatial to temporal sequence," or
"Give preview of main points."

In accomplishing the above tasks, one problem is
rapid note-taking as you listen to the speech. A good
procedure is to use scratch paper for these notes so
that you may employ your own system of abbrevia-
tions and shorthand—a little later you can translate
them to the chart, making them more meaningful and
legible.

2. You will also be assigned as the subject for another student practicing *his* listening skills. You will
find out what he thought you said (description); how
well he thought you said it (evaluation); and what he
thinks you should do to improve (prescription). You
may wish to compliment him, at least in part. However, there is often quite a difference between what
the speaker intended to say, what he thinks he said,
what the listener thinks he said, and what he actually
said (tape recorder version). If you seriously disagree
with your listener/critic, the instructor and the other
students may adjudicate. Thus the assignment provides for double and perhaps triple feedback.

**LISTENER'S REPORT
ON A STUDENT SPEAKER**

LISTENER _____ SPEAKER _____

TOPIC _____ DATE _____

I. Description	II. Evaluation

I. Description

A. Content and organization

   Opening:

   Body:

      Central idea (state fully):

      Main points (list them):

      Supports (identify a few):

   Conclusion:

B. Delivery

   Appearance:

   Body communication:

   Vocal communication:

   Language:

III. General impressions
   (Animation. Directness. Friendliness. Poise. Preparedness. Other.)

IV. Prescription
   (Suggestions for improvement: Things speaker can do.)

Speaker's comments
   (Regarding above description, evaluation, and prescription)

30

listening and critiquing
non-classroom speakers

OBJECTIVE

This project has three purposes: (1) to continue the development of purposive listening habits; (2) to observe communicative techniques that you should either use or avoid in your future speaking; and (3) to form personal standards for judging the validity and ethics of various speech communications in our society. Each of these is next briefly discussed.

BACKGROUND

Purposive listening. There is no general formula for effective listening; you need several formulas, each one tailored to your *listening purposes* in a given situation. For instance, if you attend a typical performance by Bill Cosby, Carol Burnett, or Bob Newhart, your purpose is to relax, grin, chuckle, and laugh. Your enjoyment would be killed if you sat there taking notes as you would during a lecture in your American history class. Here are most of the major purposes of listening: recreation (dinner party), learning about a topic (class lecture), getting information about a speaker (job interview), experiencing an emotional or spiritual lift (sermon), reinforcing existing beliefs (political speech by your favorite candidate), reaching a decision (debate or panel discussion), and putting a plan into overt action (briefing session). Often you have a combination of purposes, as was demonstrated by the preceding project.

If a speaker misreads the expectations that his audience brings to the meeting, he is in danger. Thus Mark Twain ruefully reported that he could not give a serious speech; no matter what he said, the listeners were looking for concealed humor and therefore they found it. You will sense that listening with a purpose —if it be inflexible, subconscious, or biased—can boomerang against the listener since he tends to hear only what he wants to hear. For example, you may listen to a political leader of the opposition party and notice only the weaknesses, overlooking obvious strengths. You should learn to listen purposively but you must be consciously aware of what you are doing and recognize the difference between listening with purpose and listening with prejudice.

Learning from example. When you are critiquing a non-classroom speaker, one of your purposes will probably differ from those of others in the audience: You will be alert for anything that might help your own improvement as a speaker. This suggests that you would be wise to seek any opportunity available in your community to hear an experienced speaker who is already successful in your chosen future vocation or profession. Students can often get access to meetings not open to the public.

Standards for making value judgments. We are bombarded in our society by seemingly countless speakers who want us to buy a product, contribute to a cause, vote a given way, sign a petition, join an organization, attend a rally, or write to our congressmen. As a student of speech communication you should not be duped by the con artists, but neither should you automatically reject every appeal—some may be worthwhile (volunteer workers for Community Chest and Red Cross always report a few instances where the discourteous citizen listens to the first sentence and immediately slams the door). What you need is a personal set of criteria by which to make dependable value judgments. You can spend an instructive half hour in the following way. Choose an "unwanted" door-to-door salesman or solicitor, invite him into the house, and ask him to tell you all about it. You then observe the sales pitch and by judicious questioning test the validity of his facts or claims and perhaps raise a few ethical issues. If you are unable to ask appropriate questions of your guest, you probably do not yet have a workable set of criteria.

In critiquing public speakers you cannot report that

you have tested them by cross-examination, but you can cross-examine yourself regarding overall value judgments of their purposes, evidence, opinions, or tactics. And it may help to discuss especially knotty problems with one or two personal friends, including those who hold opposing views. You will be assisted by referring back to pages 127-28 for our discussion of the tests of evidence and logic, and perhaps by our suggestions on pages 117-19 regarding emotional and other psychological appeals.

However, you must evolve your own most funda-mental value criteria; intelligent and sincere people often disagree. But have you ever seriously thought about the matter? For example, what about the morality of an attorney who vigorously and emotionally defends a client who he knows is guilty? What about the ethics of an evangelist who deliberately uses all the tricks of the trade in order to lure people into the church—do the ends justify the means? What about the right of free speech for extremists who strive to undermine the first amendment? And so on and on. Seek out such speaking situations for your critiques.

INSTRUCTIONS

1. Your instructor may assign one or more events to be attended and critiqued. One way of reporting is in the style of the essay, including the following sections:

a. Description of the audience and occasion. (See the first two sections of the Guide Sheet for Analyzing an Audience, pages 70-71.

b. Brief summary of the content of the speech, including a statement of the speaker's predominant purpose.

c. Discussion of your listening purposes and how well you succeeded in applying them.

d. Description of observed speaking techniques which you think you should avoid, or think you have already used effectively, or think you should try out in the future.

e. Discussion of any explicit or implicit question of the validity or ethics of what the speaker(s) said. Take a stand on the question and defend that stand.

2. Your instructor may prefer a description and evaluation to vivify what you have been practicing in your classroom talks. If so, the Criticism Chart on pages 145-46 may readily be adapted.

SUGGESTED SPEECH OCCASIONS

A jury trial
Salesmen's meeting at a local business establishment
A platform debate in a current political campaign
An intercollegiate debate
A revival meeting
A protest rally
Public lecture on controversial topic
City council meeting
Orientation meeting for new employees at a local industry
News conference of a politician or other public figure

Labor union meeting (if you belong to one)
Weekly service at a church quite different from your own denomination
Regular meeting of a community organization, such as: PTA, League of Women's Voters, Urban League, men's or women's business club, a medical or other professional society, faculty wives club, faculty senate.
NOTE: Some of the above will require permission to attend; if you know a member, perhaps you can be taken along as a guest.

five

special types of group and public communication

A cowboy riding the range during the frontier times glorified by western movies could talk to himself, his horse, or the cattle. Returning to the bunkhouse, he talked with the other cowboys and, of course, with the ranch owner's beautiful daughter. The cowboy's vocabulary, so the movies imply, consisted largely of "yup" and "nope," except for the garrulous cook called "Gabby." These stereotyped tales are valid reminders, however, that an informal communication network suffices for most of the business of living in an agrarian society.

More complex communication networks become necessities as a society becomes industrialized and mass migration into urban centers occurs. Basic types of group and public communication are supplemented by special types, many of them formalized by written sets of rules. The variety of meetings is formidable, ranging from classroom discussions among the children in elementary school to the PTA, to the local and state boards of education; politically we range from neighborhood coffee klatches to meetings of precinct workers, on up to state and national Democratic and Republican committees, plus sessions of city councils, state legislatures, and the United States Congress; and so on. Spectacular progress in electronic technology has extended the range of human vocal cords and ears, so an entire metropolis can participate in additional types of communication events. We may visualize a vast and sometimes tangled communications web of overlapping, interdependent, interlocking, and counteracting strands.

Fortunately, the complications of this web do not require a proliferation of new purposes and types of speech communication; the major purposes remain constant—to entertain, to inform, to persuade—and most of the apparently countless special types are but variations on a relatively few themes. Even the mass media become more manageable when viewed in terms of a remark by Emmy-winner, TV educator Frank Baxter, "Nobody ever talks to *an* audience of 100 million people. You talk to numerous small audiences, averaging 2.8 persons, in their own living rooms on their own terms."

Part Five contains a selection of the most common and useful special types. One underlying theme deserves critical analysis. We begin with an assignment requiring person-to-person conversations which are governed by the unwritten rule of common courtesy, "Give the other person a chance to talk." This deceptively simple communication concept evolves through the subsequent projects; you may be surprised to find that it is the basis for many of the complicated procedures of a parliamentary session conducted under Robert's Rules of Order.

31

"the grapevine":
communication networks

OBJECTIVE

This informal experiment gives firsthand experience in the communication process of horizontal diffusion of information, as contrasted with its vertical diffusion. Official pronouncements and public speeches, some of them disseminated by the mass media, do not tell the whole story of the communication network that permeate our society—receivers of these messages add an informal dimension by "talking things over" in countless conversations. The importance of these everyday person-to-person interchanges in crystallizing public opinion is often overlooked; so we will explore it.

BACKGROUND

Every major business or industry has an organizational chart with a president and board of directors at the top, with lines showing authority and responsibility moving downward through division supervisors, department foremen, leadmen, and finally to ordinary workers. Anyone who supposes that all company business communications travel up and then back down these official lines is naïve. For instance, a middle-bracket foreman with an interdepartmental problem is likely to confer directly with his peer, the foreman of the other department. News of high-level policy changes by either management or labor union may leak out and be informally discussed by practically everybody in the plant before the changes happen. In general, the type of communication that is by far the most pervasive and necessary to keep the wheels of an industry turning is person-to-person conversation at all levels of the hierarchy: at the workbench, in the conference room, on the production line, in the office, during the coffee break, or over a beer on the way home after work. This is "the grapevine"; it is much more than an exchange of gossip and rumor (although these also occur and will be discussed below).

What has just been described applies as well to other organized groups: churches, schools, government bureaus, research centers, armed services units, social clubs, or professional societies.

The foregoing practical observations are substantiated by modern research studies, some of which have focused on personal versus mass communications. These studies reveal that usually the direct effect of broadcast speeches or advertisements is surprisingly small. However, a few "opinion leaders" are likely to be stimulated to discuss their versions of some mass-media messages with family, neighbors, friends, and fellow employees. The cumulative influence of these conversations is stronger than the direct influence of the political speech or commercial ad. One attempt to summarize these findings is sociologist Paul Lazarsfeld's "two-step flow" theory: Step one is the direct (vertical) broadcast; step two is the less visible but more important (horizontal) diffusion through informal discussions sparked by unofficial opinion leaders. (See, for example, *Personal Influence* [1955] by Elihu Katz and Paul Lazarsfeld.)

In 1972, Senator Thomas Eagleton, the Democratic candidate for Vice-President, withdrew from the ticket. This unprecedented incident began when newsmen received perfectly legitimate tips regarding Eagleton's earlier hospitalizations for nervous exhaustion and mental depression. Eagleton sought to explain and justify his health history on a nationwide broadcast, but many voters speculated whether he had "told all." A few days later, a newsman named Jack Anderson broadcast by radio a completely unverified rumor that Eagleton had received traffic tickets for drunken driving. National broadcasts and other public speeches condemning this "damnable lie" did not save Eagleton. The merits of this case are not the issue here; we *do* wish to illustrate the power of grass roots discussion, even including gossip and rumor.

In summary, the role and the effectiveness of ordinary face-to-face speech communication, especially in organizational contexts, deserves more attention than it usually receives.

INSTRUCTIONS

"Have you heard the latest?" is a question that typifies the opening of many a conversation as news is being passed along the grapevine. In this project the class will informally circulate a news story among its own members in order to see what may happen despite every effort to report accurately. The instructor (or a student) will select a story from the news media or invent a fictitious one that sounds plausible. The story should deal with ongoing events, not with completed ones; for example, "further disclosures are expected and the outcome is in doubt." There should be quite a few "facts," some of which are qualified by terms such as "alleged," "unverified," and "from a usually reliable source."

The class may wish to invent its own *modus operandi* or it may use the procedure here described. The original story is taped outside of class by the instructor, and the recording is "secretly" played for two students. Each of them must relate what he has heard to at least two other class members. As soon as any member has heard the news, he passes it along to at least two more members. These conversations may occur in the hallway, at a living center, over a cup of coffee, or if necessary by telephone. After allowing a couple of days for the story to circulate, each student who has received one or more versions will record his current understanding of the story—either on tape or in complete written form. The class has now created its data; the tapes or written reports will be brought to class on the appointed day. Several or all of the tapes are played or the papers read aloud (notes on these should be taken). Then the instructor plays the tape of the original story and comparisons can be made. There is no way of predicting what will be found; the final versions may be surprisingly accurate or surprisingly inaccurate. The dynamics of the process may be analyzed by evaluating the original story and tracing its progress from person to person. What facts remained constant? How and why did omissions, additions, and modifications creep in? Distortions due to bias or malice may be revealed and probed. Hopefully, no one will burlesque the story as a gag—but even that can be traced and evaluated. Another provocative result may be that some of the class received several versions but a few members were not contacted at all—why, and why not? And a final thought: maybe the *real* grapevine is now starting, with this project as the "story."

32

speech of introduction

OBJECTIVE

The aim of this project is to offer practical experience in introducing a principal speaker to his audience. A unique feature of a speech of introduction is that you seek to direct attention away from yourself.

BACKGROUND

You have been nominated to introduce the speaker of the meeting. The occasion may be the annual banquet of your firm or the weekly meeting of a discussion group, a women's club, or an honorary society. Business, professional, civic, and cultural groups frequently hear guest speakers, and responsibility for the introduction this time is yours. Immediately comes a flurry of questions: What shall I say? What should I avoid saying? How long should I talk? How much of his subject should I describe? This assignment places you at the head table and asks that you effectively present the main speaker to his audience.

Your speaker has a right to expect as friendly and as interested an audience as it is in your power to offer him. Your basic purpose is to create in the audience a desire to hear the speaker. Interest in the speaker and topic must be aroused, and you will aim to make the audience both like and respect your guest.

A successful speech of introduction begins with understanding or familiarity with the speaker and his topic. Don't be satisfied with a mere collection of facts about the speaker's life and career. Try to discover incidents and episodes in the speaker's background that reveal him as a warm and capable human being. Rather than simply saying that the speaker is "honest" or "courageous," relate instances from his career that suggest honesty and courage. Conclusions drawn by the audience itself are more persuasive than your inventory of the speaker's attributes could be. In describing the life of your guest, avoid a detailed catalogue of dates and accomplishments. Select milestones in his life. The audience is most interested in the qualifications and experiences that uniquely equip him to address them on this subject.

In your speech of introduction, resist the temptation to talk about yourself or to explain your views on the subject. Irvin S. Cobb once described his distress as a witless chairman elaborated upon Cobb's theme for over half an hour. "It was," reported Cobb, "a somewhat condensed but on the whole satisfactory version of my speech." The introducer obviously should limit himself to emphasis on the importance of the speaker's theme, and he should stress the value to this particular audience of information and ideas the speaker will offer. Mention of the appropriateness of speaker or subject to this occasion or audience contributes to sharpened audience interest.

Humor may be employed effectively in the speech of introduction. Contrived jokes of the "this reminds me of a story" variety seldom achieve the response that spontaneous humor arising from the occasion can evoke. But if suitable to the occasion and in good taste, humor is especially effective in the speech of introduction, since both speakers and audiences seem to welcome a chance to relax in an atmosphere of informality. Whatever stories or anecdotes are used should contribute to the audience's favorable impression of the speaker. He hardly would appreciate your making him look foolish as the butt of some ill-considered humor; but he would welcome meeting his audience in the friendly attitude that good-natured humor will stimulate.

The speech of introduction can suffer much more from excessive length than from brevity. You—and don't ever forget—are not the featured speaker of the day but rather a spotlight focusing the listeners' attention upon the guest. When President Eisenhower was introduced by the spellbinding oratory of a long-winded governor, he remarked to an aide, "This is like sending the bat boy in after Babe Ruth." Far better, in this circumstance, was Shailer Mathews' introduction of Woodrow Wilson: "Ladies and Gentlemen, the President."

INSTRUCTIONS

Any reasonably true-to-life situation in which you might introduce a speaker can be utilized in this assignment. Persons such as the following often are introduced to campus or to business, professional, and civic groups:

news commentator	politician
scientist	student leader
alumnus	labor leader
writer	professional lecturer
world traveler	foreign correspondent
artist	advertising executive
sports celebrity	educator
missionary	company president
diplomat	military spokesman

The shelves of biographies in your neighborhood or school library will provide much of the background you need for this speech. Biographical dictionaries may be used for quick confirmation of career details. Do not overlook the general and specialized guides to periodical literature, as they can point to recent articles on the speaker of your choice. Or if the person you select to introduce is not a figure of national or international prominence, but is well known only locally, interviews can provide firsthand information. Our main stress here is the necessity of immersing yourself in the speaker's biography, whether formal or informal.

The speech itself, usually only two to four minutes in length, should build to the interest climax as you turn to the speaker, announcing his name and topic and presenting him to the hearers much as you would introduce him to a group of friends in your own house.

NAME _____ DATE _____

AUDIENCE AND OCCASION _____

PERSON BEING INTRODUCED _____

Opening   1   2   3   4   5

Was the hypothetical occasion plausible?

Did the opening remarks set an appropriate atmosphere?

Did the opening remarks lead smoothly into the introduction itself?

Body   1   2   3   4   5

Did the introducer "humanize" his speaker?

Did the introducer make the audience want to hear the speaker?

Did the introducer overpraise the speaker?

Did the introducer state the speaker's subject properly?

Was interest aroused in the topic?

Was the topic accurately announced?

Did the introducer "steal the speaker's thunder" by saying too much about the topic?

Conclusion   1   2   3   4   5

Were the final words climactic?

Did the introducer lead the applause?

Did the introducer remain standing until the speaker reached the lectern?

Comments on delivery:

33

welcomes, farewells, and presentations

OBJECTIVE

This project will provide opportunity to practice and to hear several types of "occasional speeches" or "speeches for special occasions." Such talks are usually, although not always, given as part of a luncheon or banquet program. For your future use, some suggestions on how to run a banquet are given on pages 158–59.

BACKGROUND

Professional, political, social, and other types of organizations are constantly holding conventions, banquets, or rallies. Much of the speechmaking at these affairs is covered elsewhere in this guidebook—panels, symposia, visual demonstrations, information talks, and so on. Frequently, however, there are speeches of welcome or farewell, presentations of gifts or awards, speeches of response; these are the most common examples of what are often called "speeches for special occasions."

Speeches for special occasions have several unique characteristics: they are shorter than most other speeches; the audience usually knows beforehand the speaker's purpose and where his remarks will lead; and the talks have certain established requisites of content. These guiding features mean that occasional speeches require particular attention to their composition and delivery. They should almost never include a discussion of controversial questions. Usually such speeches are best guided by the old adage, "Tell them what they want to hear." Another good rule of thumb is, "Give them a mixture of sentiment and humor." A more technical way of stating the foregoing speech purposes is this: reinforce existing audience attitudes.

INSTRUCTIONS

The instructor will divide the class into groups of three or four. Each group should meet separately to plan a program. The first step is to agree upon a theme. The instructor will probably require that several common types of program and theme be represented. The chosen situation should be plausible; do not burlesque or satirize. Some possibilities are as follows:

1. **Welcome to an individual.** The Chamber of Commerce may give a welcoming banquet to an important person who is paying a visit to the city.
2. **Welcome to a group.** The president or dean of the college may extend a welcome to the members of a state or regional professional society who are holding their annual convention on this campus.
3. **Farewell to an individual.** Management and employees have gathered to honor a colleague who is retiring after thirty years of service.

4. **Presentation of a gift.** Former students celebrate the twenty-fifth year of teaching of a favorite teacher.
5. **Presentation of an award.** A high school senior class holds its annual banquet at which awards are given to winners of scholastic or other competition.

Specific hints for each of the several kinds of talks:

Welcome. The general mood should be cordial, happy, sincere. Touch upon the welcoming theme early, usually in the first sentence. You have three things to talk about: the person or organization being welcomed, the hosts, and the occasion. Praise all three of them. Restate the welcome in closing. If you are welcoming a group, predict or wish them success in their meetings.

Farewell. The general mood should be a mixture of happiness and regret. Materials usually are drawn from the following: your mixed feelings at leaving, your past associations with the group, your hope of maintaining contacts with friends, and your continued good wishes.

Presentation. The mood should be regulated by the occasion. You may talk about the recipient of the gift or winner of the award, the gift or award itself, the occasion, and sometimes the losers. If the occasion is an annual affair, you may wish to give a brief history of it. In praising the recipient or winner, do not overdo your praise—the poor fellow has to respond. Often your compliments should be tempered with humor. Stress the symbolic value of the gift or award. If the presentation follows a contest, be sure to praise the losers. Plan your talk so that the climax comes at the end with the making of the presentation.

Response. In responding to an introduction, a welcome, or a presentation, you dare not bluntly reject praise or smugly accept it—the keynote is tact. Your words should reflect your happiness, gratitude, and modesty. The best solution usually is to reply to praise with praise. You can praise the group as a whole or individual members of it; you can praise the occasion and the gift or award; you can praise colleagues or opponents.

HOW TO RUN A BANQUET

A well-managed banquet moves along smoothly, efficiently, and pleasantly. A poorly managed banquet staggers from one mishap to another; people arrive too early or late because of a mix-up in advance announcements or publicity; guests loiter in the lobby for twenty wasted minutes before someone finally remembers to lead the way toward the tables; they stand there uncertainly wondering when to be seated; the service is slow; the chicken and potatoes are cold; the program starts more than an hour late with some inappropriate or unnecessary entertainment; the program drags; too many people are introduced; the toastmaster's jokes are stale; there are too many speakers and they all talk too long; the room becomes unbearably hot and stuffy; and the guests greet the ending with relief (except for the few bold ones who escape an hour early through the side door).

Ordinarily, better coordination results when there is only one committee, thus centering final authority and responsibility in one chairman. The chairman should assign specific duties to all committee members; if possible, he should consult early regarding proposed plans with the person who is to be toastmaster or master of ceremonies.

The choice of a hotel or restaurant should not be based entirely upon menus and prices; acoustics, ventilation, and table arrangements should also be considered. There should be enough kitchen help and waitresses to ensure fast and efficient service.

Avoid setting up a public address system unless one is absolutely necessary. In the latter situation, be sure a reliable operator is present to adjust the equipment when it breaks down, crackles, or screeches (as it always does).

A careful time schedule, based upon realistic estimates for all of the items, should be prepared. Ways and means of tactfully enforcing the schedule should be decided; for example, all speakers or entertainers should kindly but firmly be told of their time limits.

In planning the program the committee should know what to *exclude*. A naïve committee wants everything: some group singing, a piano solo, a tap dance by a local youngster, introductions of ten special guests, introductions of officers and committee members, announcement of coming events, several preliminary speakers, and at long last the principal speaker. Unless precautions are taken, everything is likely to run longer than expected. Thus the song leader is asked to warm up the audience by leading them through one or two lively songs. But he makes a production of it. Result? Instead of about five minutes, he takes thirty-two.

On the night of the banquet get the guests to the tables on time—if the master of ceremonies and the club president lead the way, the others will follow. While the guests are finding their places the master of ceremonies should be alert to the danger of an awkward interval of uncertainty about when to sit down. If someone has been asked to say grace, he should show by example (and if necessary by a gesture) that everyone is to remain standing. If a grace is not to be said, he should wait until a majority have reached their places, then say to the several nearest people, "Shall we be seated?" This will signal the whole group.

The master of ceremonies should start the program on time (even if he is forced to overlap the dessert and coffee). If guests or members are to be introduced, remember that after about the fourth, applause becomes increasingly perfunctory. Often you can introduce them by groups: "Let me present the committee who planned this banquet. As I call their names will they please rise. Please hold your applause until all five are standing." The master of ceremonies should keep the program moving, which usually means that he should keep his own remarks brief and to the point. He should do everything possible to end it on time. When the final speaker has concluded, the master of ceremonies should compliment him in one sentence; then clearly announce, "This meeting is adjourned."

NAME _____ DATE _____

Introduction   1   2   3   4   5

   Did the speaker refer to the chairman's remarks?

   Did he refer to the occasion?

   Was the hypothetical occasion plausible?

   Was the opening appropriate?

Body   1   2   3   4   5

   Did the speaker give appropriate praise to the recipient?

   Was the praise overdone?

   Were there enough illustrative supports, such as anecdotes, instances, quotations?

Conclusion   1   2   3   4   5

   Did the final words round off the talk?

   Did the conclusion focus attention on the main theme?

   Was the conclusion climactic?

Delivery   1   2   3   4   5

   Visual:

   Vocal:

   Verbal:

33 CRITICISM CHART
RESPONSE OR ACCEPTANCE

NAME _____ DATE _____

Introduction   1   2   3   4   5

Did the opening words express sincere thanks?

Did the speaker refer to remarks by previous speakers?

Did he refer to the occasion?

Was the hypothetical occasion plausible?

Was the opening appropriate?

Body   1   2   3   4   5

Did the speaker reply to praise tactfully, by returning praise, by sharing credit with others?

Were there enough illustrative supports, such as anecdotes, instances, quotations?

Conclusion   1   2   3   4   5

Did the final words round off the talk?

Did the speaker restate his appreciation?

Delivery   1   2   3   4   5

Visual:

Vocal:

Verbal:

34

panel discussion

OBJECTIVE

The purposes of this project are (1) to introduce you to basic rules and techniques of panel discussion, and (2) to give you practical experience in leadership and participation in a group decision-making activity.

BACKGROUND

You have frequently engaged in informal discussions with groups of friends or acquaintances. Occasionally you have served on committees. Probably you have participated from time to time in other types of small-group discussion. One of these types is called panel discussion. Its versatility is demonstrated by the variety of radio and television panels and talk shows. You are about to take part in a panel discussion before the other members of your class; you will have an opportunity to listen critically to several other panels.

A panel may be roughly defined as an informal small-group discussion which takes place before an audience. Its chief purposes usually are problem solving and information dissemination. The effectiveness of a panel is, therefore, measured in terms of audience response. The success of your panel will be judged by how well you arouse the interest of class members in your topic, by whether you can give them new information and new viewpoints about your topic, and by how well you advance their thinking toward solution of your problem.

To be effective in providing information and alternatives, a good panel discussion needs an agenda or overall plan known to the participants. Consider the following pattern in organizing your discussion.

I. Formulation of the problem
   A. What is the problem? What are its limits?
   B. What is the meaning of terms used to state the problem?

II. Analysis of the problem
   A. Description and diagnosis
      1. What are the symptoms or observable effects of the problem?
      2. What are the causes or factors producing these effects?
      3. What are the obstacles to solution?
   B. Determination of goals
      1. What are the criteria by which solutions are to be measured?
      2. What is the priority of the criteria or goals and the relative weight attached to them?
      3. Are the goals desirable and attainable?

III. Consideration of alternative proposals
   A. What are the possible solutions to the problem?
   B. Appraisal of suggested solutions
      1. What will be the consequences of adopting each proposal?
      2. What are the relative merits of the proposals in meeting criteria or goals?
      3. What are the advantages and disadvantages of each proposal?

IV. Plan of action
   A. What can be done to test the solution concluded to be the best?
   B. What steps would need to be taken to put the proposed solution into operation?

INSTRUCTIONS

The class will be divided into groups of five or six each. The instructor will announce time limits and dates. For example, he may wish to hear one panel per meeting, allowing forty to fifty minutes for each panel.

Each group will hold a planning meeting and will

begin by electing one of its members as chairman. Its second task will be to choose a discussion topic. Topics should be timely, controversial, and interesting. You should come prepared to suggest one or more topics that you would like to discuss or hear discussed. Each group should then agree upon a general outline of points in the order in which they will be discussed. Agreement also should be reached regarding time limits and procedures. A group should not try to rehearse its discussion; such rehearsals almost invariably kill the spontaneity of the actual program.

Following the planning session, you should do as much reading as possible about the topic. On the appointed day you should come prepared to support your position with facts, figures, and authorities. (Check the tests of evidence on page 127.) The discussion itself should be a lively give-and-take during which the members of the panel are literally thinking aloud, each person constantly adapting his remarks to what the others have said.

Here are suggestions for effective participation. If you are chairman of your group, your duties are as follows:

1. Open the program with a brief statement introducing panel members and their topic.

2. Get the discussion started in accordance with an advance plan.
3. Keep the discussion moving by means of questions or other devices.
4. Give all members of the panel an equal opportunity to talk.
5. Remain neutral on the topic; act as an impartial moderator during disputes.
6. Guide the discussion in terms of a prearranged outline.
7. Watch the time limits.
8. Close the program with a brief summarizing statement.

If you are a participant other than the chairman, your duties are as follows:

1. Secure recognition from the chairman when you want to speak.
2. Have something worthwhile to say.
3. Keep your remarks brief and to the point.
4. You may use notes, but do not make set speeches.
5. Address your discussion primarily to the other members of the panel, but talk loudly enough for the rest of the audience to hear.
6. Express your own views honestly and vigorously, but be fair in allowing others to express theirs.
7. Abide by the chairman's decisions with good grace.

SUGGESTED TOPICS

Each panel should, of course, have a different topic from the other panels. The following list is suggestive only; you may think of a better topic for your group.

What should be done to control pollution of rivers and lakes?

What changes are most needed in our secondary schools?

How should the federal government administer its program of financial aid to college students?

What should be the foreign aid program of the United States?

Can we improve our methods of selecting presidential candidates?

To what extent can a scientist be religious?

How effective is student government on this campus?

How can TV advertising be improved?

What should be America's role in the Middle East?

What ethical standards should the public demand of candidates for public office?

What should be the policy on this campus regarding national social fraternities?

What should be done to prevent the hijacking of aircraft?

35

symposium

OBJECTIVE

A symposium is a program of three or more speeches, each of which develops a different aspect or side of a central theme or common problem. This assignment will provide practice in planning and presenting such a program.

BACKGROUND

Notice some resemblances and differences between a symposium and a panel. Both require three or more participants representing divergent points of view upon a single topic. In a panel, as you will recall, the topic is subdivided into its main points, and each point is discussed in give-and-take fashion by all the participants before proceeding to the next point. In a symposium, however, the discussion of the topic is organized in terms of viewpoints rather than subpoints, and each viewpoint is presented by one participant in a prepared speech. Both the symposium and the panel have virtues, and in choosing between them the decision should hinge upon the nature of the topic, the characteristics of the audience or occasion, and the abilities of the available participants.

One virtue of the symposium method is that equal opportunity and equal time may be given to each participant. If a symposium is well planned and well presented, the series of talks should provide the audience with a coherent, unified picture—a mosaic of interrelated information and opinions; there should be almost no overlap or repetition of materials among the speakers. Although the members of a symposium may be presenting opposing points of view, they should work together as a team to fulfill their joint responsibility of providing the audience with a unified program.

Essentially the symposium is a form of public discussion. To provide for maximum interaction among the participants, therefore, a symposium is usually followed by an open forum period, the time for which is flexible and may be contracted or expanded to conform with apparent audience interest.

INSTRUCTIONS

The class will be divided into symposium groups, each consisting of from three to five speakers and a chairman. Each chairman will arrange to meet with his group as early as possible before the program to choose a topic and to decide upon a systematic plan of attack. As soon as a topic has been chosen your group must decide upon what aspects or viewpoints should be presented, and in what sequence. Most topics can be organized for a symposium in any of several different ways; review these possibilities and try to choose the best one. Do not adjourn your meeting until a firm agreement has been reached, for without a definite advance plan your program is likely to be a disappointment to both your group and the audience.

In planning, your group may wish to develop a central *theme*. For instance, the theme might be, "The Movie Industry." One division of this theme into aspects or phases might be (1) the recreational, (2) the educational, and (3) the financial. Your group may instead wish to develop a common *problem* with three or more sides, for example, how to meet medical expenses. One speaker might open the program with an analysis of the problem, describing the high costs of medical care, the difficulties of budgeting doctors' bills, and the like. Three other speakers might advocate respectively (1) private practice and individual payment, (2) voluntary health insurance, and (3) medical care at public expense. You can probably think of other possible ways of organizing either of the above examples. Whatever the scheme or arrangement, be sure that there is an observable relationship among the talks. During the program, reference to each other's remarks helps to create a sense of continuity that marks a worthwhile symposium.

The chairman occupies a position of special responsibility. He helps in the planning stage, working closely with the group in the choice and wording of the topic, and guiding the group toward an agreement upon an organizational scheme. He supervises the physical preparation of the meeting place. During the program itself he opens the meeting with a brief introductory statement stressing the significance and timeliness of the topic, introduces speakers and their topics, provides transitional remarks, moderates the open forum period, and finally presents a concluding statement and adjourns the meeting.

SUGGESTED TOPICS

As already indicated, a good symposium topic may be either a central theme with three or more aspects, or it may be a common problem with three or more sides.

What should be done about juvenile delinquency?
The censorship codes of the motion picture, radio, and television industries
Why can't Johnny read?
Our foreign trade

Should early marriages be encouraged?
The causes of war
Why go to church?
How can we control inflation?
What should be the objectives of United States foreign policy?
The vital issues before Congress today
How can we strengthen the United Nations?
The mainsprings of national economic progress
Consumer protection
But is it music?

36

open forum

OBJECTIVE

The overall aim of an open forum is to secure orderly audience participation in a public meeting. This project furnishes practice in chairmanship, platform presentation, and participation from the floor.

BACKGROUND

The term "open forum" is here used to denote a method for public discussion, suitable for selected occasions, that restricts audience participation to questions and brief comments.

An open forum cannot be conducted all by itself—it must be preceded by some other type of program, such as a lecture, debate, panel, or symposium. The amount and type of response from the floor is restricted, but for good reasons. For example, when the attendance is large it is better to get 20 or 25 brief questions and answers rather than two or three lengthy harangues. Perhaps the principal speaker is an acknowledged authority, and questions are the best way to get him to clarify or elaborate. Or the speaker has sought to influence beliefs or get action, and probing questions may test possible weaknesses in his facts or logic.

The dynamics of an open forum may be best studied by analyzing the tasks of the chairman which are listed in the left-hand column of the chart on page 170. The first step, often overlooked, is to establish a few ground rules before asking for the first questions. The most important rule is that questions are addressed to a speaker *through* the chairman. For emphasis, the chairman should restate the first question before signaling the speaker to answer. Psychologically, this rule is the chairman's technique for maintaining orderliness and control. So long as the forum is proceeding smoothly, he needs only to maintain his status by rewording questions that are obviously poorly stated or by occasionally gesturing to suggest that he is passing along the question. But sometimes the going gets rough and he must promptly reestablish "who's in charge here."

Sometimes getting the first question from an audience is like getting the first olive from the jar; at other times, audiences may be too vociferous. The chairman must quickly sense such problems and adapt promptly; possible techniques are indicated for either type of audience in the right-hand column of the chart.

Hopefully, the remainder of the chart is self-explanatory. Perhaps you will notice that the function of the chairman is to *direct* the open forum. Figuratively, his job is like that of a traffic officer at a street intersection where there are no automatic signals in operation. He must direct the flow of traffic in accordance with his immediate observation and judgment: he holds back some motorists, encourages others to proceed and points out the directions in which they may proceed; he prevents U turns or other such maneuvers; he adapts to a stalled car or other unexpected incident. Likewise, the chairman of the open forum must direct the flow of questions, comments, and replies.

INSTRUCTIONS

Your instructor will specify the presentations that will precede the open forum periods. The programs may be new ones planned especially for the forum exercise. Or the instructor may combine the open forum assignments with one or more previous projects, such as the informative, persuasive, or argumentative speeches; the open forum is often effective in conjunction with a panel discussion or symposium.

Chairmen will of course be appointed and time limits specified. The instructor may secretly arrange for some of the participants to deliberately create typical open forum problems in order to show how naturally and even insidiously they may intrude themselves. Of course, such problems intentionally put the chairman on the spot as he attempts to cope with them.

The chart below can do double duty: (1) as a checklist to guide a prospective chairman, and (2) as a **Criticism Chart** for a specific performance. Criticisms can usually be indicated by brief notations (O.K., overdone, needed this, etc.), with perhaps arrows pointing to the appropriate items.

CHAIRMANSHIP OF OPEN FORUMS

What the Chairman Does	*Methods He May Use*
1. State the rules	1. State them in detail 2. Sketch them as brief reminders
2. Get first questions started	1. General enthusiasm of mood and manner 2. Ask first question himself 3. Plant a "stooge" 4. Ask specific individuals for questions
3. Encourage maximum participation	1. One question per person so long as others want the floor 2. Distribute questions throughout the auditorium 3. Not more than 3 consecutive questions to one speaker in multispeaker programs 4. Have speakers answer briefly 5. Help questioners express themselves: restate poorly worded questions or indistinct ones 6. Do not hold reins of authority too tightly
4. Protect speaker(s)	1. Overrule personal questions, or those otherwise malicious or unfair 2. Restate difficult questions to give speaker a moment to think
5. Keep questioners in control	1. Refer to self as "the Chair," not as "I" 2. Remind questioners to secure recognition 3. Restate questions occasionally 4. Cut in on "crackpots" trying to orate 5. Cut in if questioner tries to start a dialogue with speaker 6. Do not be too permissive
6. Close the forum properly	1. Close it while questions are still pending 2. Establish and stay within time limits 3. Close with brief statement of progress made 4. Thank the speaker(s) and audience and signal clearly when program is ended

37

parliamentary session

OBJECTIVE

A club or organization is a group of individuals banded together for a common purpose. To ensure democratic conduct of their affairs, as well as order and efficiency, they employ principles of parliamentary procedure. This section will (1) acquaint you with standard parliamentary procedures, and (2) thrust you directly into a decision-making session for firsthand experience in an organized meeting.

BACKGROUND

Probably when you first attended the meeting of a club or organization at which business was conducted, you heard unfamiliar words and phrases and noticed an apparently set formula for the program. The procedure may have seemed complicated and stilted, and the business handled with surprising speed or agonizing delay. As a bewildered outsider, you may have felt that you were watching experts play some esoteric game. But the principles of parliamentary law are relatively simple, and their applications are anchored in common sense. Here are the basic principles:

1. The will of the majority should prevail.
2. The minority deserves a chance to be heard.
3. Definite decisions should be made after free discussion.
4. Business should be transacted in an orderly manner.
5. Each member has equal rights and obligations.
6. Only one question can be considered at a time.
7. The presiding officer must be strictly impartial.

Careful study of these principles should not be slighted simply because, at first reading, the statements seem self-evident. Like the principles of democratic government itself, they are basic ways of achieving what Thomas Jefferson called "equal and exact justice for all men." Thorough understanding of the basic principles of parliamentary law will simplify and clarify your study of detailed handbooks. Mastery of these principles will help you, even in the stress of an actual meeting, to resolve questions involving complicated details; doing the right thing is usually the right thing to do. View parliamentary law as a reasonable code of ethics for working together—the rules of the game for conducting organizational business.

Occasionally one hears the smug statement: "That is not according to Robert's Rules of Order." While this comment may stop discussion, it should not intimidate. Each club or organization may set up its own rules of conduct. They may be outlandish, but every organization has a right to determine the code under which it will exist. To supplement organizational codes, the club may add a statement that in all matters not covered in their constitution and bylaws, Robert's Rules of Order shall prevail, or, indeed, that any one from a dozen other codes of parliamentary procedure shall prevail. In other words, there is no official set of rules that you must follow exactly and in all cases. But an organization is well advised to accept some widely used set of rules and to modify procedure to meet its own needs.

INSTRUCTIONS

The best way to learn the practice of parliamentary procedure is to practice it. This assignment culminates in an actual parliamentary session or may be extended to several sessions. We have included the basic organization of a parliamentary meeting, a table of parliamentary motions showing precedence (pronounced pre CEED′ ence) and characteristics of each, and the proper phrasing of common motions. The table of motions on page 174 should be carefully studied for precedence, which simply means the priority of one motion over another. Notice that while all business starts with a main motion, all other motions take priority over it. The meeting ends with the motion to adjourn which takes priority over everything. This subject of precedence deserves class discussion before the opening session, because it is fundamental to your grasp of parliamentary law.

The following instructions can serve as a model for your parliamentary session:

I. Time and place
   A. The meeting will start promptly at 10 A.M.
   B. All sessions will be held in Founder's Hall, Room 433
II. Election of officers
   A. The first session (see below) includes the election of a presiding officer, secretary, and sergeant at arms; and the appointment of a parliamentarian
   B. Duties of officers
     1. President—presides at the session
     2. Secretary—keeps records of the session
     3. Parliamentarian—serves as chairman's adviser on procedural matters
     4. Sergeant at arms—assists in maintaining order during the session
   C. Members who nominate officers may give nominating speeches not to exceed two minutes
III. Agenda for first session
   A. Opening of the meeting
   B. Election of officers
   C. Introduction of resolutions
   D. Debate and action on resolutions
   E. Adjournment
IV. Agenda for subsequent sessions
   A. Call to order
   B. Reading minutes of previous meeting
   C. Reports of standing and special committees
   D. Unfinished business
   E. New business
   F. Announcements
   G. Adjournment
V. Special Rules for the sessions
   A. A copy of each resolution will be given to the secretary.
   B. Member who introduces the resolution is allowed to speak first and last upon it.
   C. Speeches on resolutions are limited to two minutes.
   D. No member may speak a second time until all others desiring to speak have done so.

The Brief Table of Parliamentary Motions, which includes those most frequently used, will govern your meeting. A temporary chairman will serve until

officers are elected; they take office immediately. The presiding officer, to preserve impartiality, is addressed as "Mr. Chairman"; he refers to himself as "the Chair." Typical phrasing of eight common motions shows how members and chairman word their remarks:

Main motion. "Mr. Chairman [wait for recognition by the Chair], I move adoption of the following resolution—Resolved: That this organization. . . [state your motion]." Or "I move that this organization. . ." Without waiting for recognition by the Chair, another member simply says, "I second it." After the second, the Chair calls for discussion: "It has been moved and seconded that this organization. . . Is there any discussion?"

The orderly disposition of any main motion requires the following steps:
1. Rise and address the chairman.
2. Be recognized by chairman.
3. State your motion.
4. Another member seconds it.
5. Chairman states motion to group.
6. Motion is debated (and amended if necessary).
7. Motion is voted upon by group.

Amendment. To change the wording of a motion to a more desirable form, say, "Mr. Chairman [wait for recognition], I move to amend the resolution by striking out the words. . ." Or ". . . by inserting the words. . ." Or ". . . by adding the words. . ." If features of an amendment should be changed: "Mr. Chairman, I move to amend the amendment by. . ."

Previous question. After recognition: "Mr. Chairman, I move the previous question." Chairman: "It has been moved and seconded to vote immediately on the motion before the group. Those in favor of voting immediately, please rise. Be seated. Those opposed, please rise. Be seated. The motion to vote immediately is carried. Those in favor of the main motion [state it] say, 'Aye.'"

Parliamentary inquiry. If you need information on parliamentary procedure, you can say, "Mr. Chairman, I rise to a parliamentary inquiry." Chairman: "State your inquiry." Proposer: "Is an amendment to this motion in order?" Or you may ask, "Mr. Chairman, I rise for information. May I ask the speaker a question?"

Point of order. If you think that the Chair is mistaken in its procedure, you can say, "I rise to a point of order." The Chair then asks you to state your point of order: "The Chair is out of order in permitting Art Guyer to speak when Del King has the floor." Chairman: "Your point of order is well taken. Will Mr. Guyer please be seated?"

Lay on the table. If you wish to have the pending question set aside temporarily because something more urgent has arisen, you can say, "Mr. Chairman,

I move that the motion be laid on the table." Chairman: "It has been moved and seconded to lay the motion on the table. There is no discussion. All those in favor of tabling, say 'Aye.' Those opposed, say 'No.' The motion is carried. The question is tabled." [Later, a motion can be made to take from the table.]

Postpone indefinitely. If your intention is to suppress or kill a motion without letting it come to a vote, the proper wording is: "Mr. Chairman, I move that the motion to. . . be postponed indefinitely." Chairman: "It has been moved and seconded to postpone indefinitely the motion before us. Is there any discussion? . . . All those in favor of postponing indefinitely, say 'Aye.' Those opposed say 'No.' The motion is defeated. Discussion of the main motion will continue."

Refer to committee. If you think that the proposal should be turned over to a small, specialized group for study and recommendation, you can say, "Mr. Chairman, I move to refer the motion to the Finance Committee to report at our next meeting." Chairman: "It has been moved and seconded to refer the motion to the Finance Committee. Any discussion? . . . All in favor of referring the question, say 'Aye.' Those opposed, say 'No.' The motion is carried. The question is referred to the Finance Committee whose report will be made at our next meeting."

BRIEF TABLE OF PARLIAMENTARY MOTIONS

These motions are listed in order of rank: the lowest in rank is listed first (except incidental motions, which have no order of precedence among themselves).

MOTION	USUAL PURPOSE	INTERRUPT SPEAKER?	REQUIRE SECOND?	DEBATABLE?	AMENDABLE?	VOTE REQUIRED?
I *Main Motion*	To introduce business.	No	Yes	Yes	Yes	Maj.
II *Subsidiary Motions:*	Used to modify or dispose of the main motion.					
Postpone indefinitely	To suppress consideration of main motion	No	Yes	Yes	No	Maj.
Amend	To change a resolution	No	Yes	Yes	Yes	Maj.
Refer to committee	For study and recommendations	No	Yes	Yes	Yes	Maj.
Postpone definitely	To postpone to a certain time	No	Yes	Yes	Yes	Maj.
Previous question	To vote immediately	No	Yes	No	No	2/3
Lay on the table	To lay pending question aside temporarily	No	Yes	No	No	Maj.
III *Incidental Motions:*	Pertain to the motions being considered.					
Parliamentary inquiry	To learn procedure or information	Yes	No	No	No	None
Point of order	To correct a parliamentary error	Yes	No	No	No	None
Withdrawal of motion	Remove motion from consideration	No	No	No	No	Maj.
Division of assembly	To secure an accurate vote	Yes	No	No	No	None
Division of a question	To divide motion for separate consideration	No	Yes	No	Yes	Maj.
Appeal decision of the chair	To reverse ruling of the chair	Yes	Yes	No	No	Maj.
IV *Privileged Motions:*	Do not pertain to pending motions, but to the members.					
Question of privilege	Comfort or convenience of members	Yes	No	No	No	None
Recess	For a brief intermission	No	Yes	No	Yes	Maj.
Adjourn	Dismiss session	No	Yes	No	No	Maj.

38

biography speech

OBJECTIVE

This project deals with the biographies or autobiographies of famous or unusual people. The principal purpose of the project is to allow you to practice in a single speech as many as possible of the principles that have been separately emphasized during this term. Review the table of contents to remind yourself of the ground to be covered.

BACKGROUND

The most important criterion for judging your work in this course is your improvement as a speech communicator. Consequently, most instructors assign special significance to your final speech. How does it compare with your previous performances dating back to the first few meetings of the class? The biography talk may be used earlier in the term but it is a well-tried final speaking assignment: (1) The use of a common theme helps to make all of the talks somewhat easier to view comparatively and in perspective; when considered in toto the talks constitute a single "program," albeit a mosaic type; (2) The project requires an adequate background of research; you draw upon a reservoir of material, only a small portion of which can be presented within your time limits; (3) The nature of the materials permits the instructor to specify almost any speech purpose or type—to inform, to reinforce attitudes or beliefs (to stimulate), to build attitudes (to convince), to release attitudes (to actuate), or to influence audience be-

havior through some other variation of persuasive speaking; (4) Optimum flexibility is offered to each student for emphasizing almost any aspect of speech communication; your imagination and originality are challenged beginning with the first step, which is of course your choice of a person as your subject.

Biography talks are probably more common than you realize since they are usually called by other names. You have already given one or more abbreviated versions: speeches of introduction, welcome, farewell, or presentation of an award. Examples of fuller treatment include nominating speeches ("the man who"), eulogies, commemorations, sometimes lectures and dedication ceremonies, and sometimes other occasions, such as a commencement. Each of the latter examples permits practice in speech principles and techniques beyond the ordinary basics; they permit you to demonstrate a representative sample of what you have learned during the course. So make good use of the opportunity.

INSTRUCTIONS

Choose as a subject the life of some important or unusual man or woman. The man or woman must be one about whom a book has been written or about whom an equivalent amount of material is available. Your choice should be thoughtful and imaginative. You might select one from your chosen future field of work. For example, if you are a prelaw student, you might profitably study the life of Oliver Wendell Holmes or Thurgood Marshall. On the other hand, you might select someone from a field altogether dif-

ferent from your major. For example, if you are an engineering student, you might broaden yourself by becoming acquainted with the life of a great artist, poet, musician, or ballerina. Or you might make a purely personal choice—someone who is for you a hero, a villain, or an enigma.

After the instructor's approval of your subject and the biographical book, you begin reading; do this at least two weeks prior to the date you are to give the talk. As you read, be alert for supporting materials:

anecdotes, quotations, explanations, descriptions, instances, and visual aids.

Your next important task is to narrow the subject. You are speaking from a reservoir of knowledge; it is impossible to present all you know in eight minutes or even eighty, nor should you want to try. In deciding the best way to narrow the topic, depend heavily upon analysis of your classmates, most of whom you should know pretty well by this time. You are seeking a theme or focus that will interest you and simultaneously coincide with or at least overlap the predicted interest of your listeners. This narrowed topic becomes the central idea for your talk. Word it carefully as a complete sentence; you may need to revise this central idea several times or even completely discard it in favor of a better idea as you accomplish this crucial step in your preparation.

You are now ready to construct your outline in accordance with suggestions made in various preceding projects. Be sure to include at least five different forms of support. Avoid falling into the trap of simple chronology, merely listing a monotonous procession of dates that reveals no more about the individual than a recitation of cities and mileages tells about an auto trip from Los Angeles to Chicago; we may be impressed that it was a long, tough journey, but the central idea gets lost in a maze of names and numbers.

Record a clear copy of your outline on the form on pages 177-78. Read carefully the Criticism Chart that follows on pages 179-80.

38 OUTLINE OF BIOGRAPHY SPEECH

NAME _____ **DATE** _____

TOPIC _____

BOOK OR ARTICLES READ _____

_____

Build this outline in accordance with the instructions just given; review suggestions and models in Project 9 on pages 29–33.

Outline of biography speech, continued

NAME_____ DATE_____

TOPIC_____

Content

Introduction   1   2   3   4   5

    Was opening interesting?

    Was it appropriate?

    Did it lead smoothly into body of speech?

Body   1   2   3   4   5

    Was there a single central idea?

    Was central idea clear enough?

    Were there two to five main points?

    Were the main points interrelated?

    Were the several speech units well organized?   Statements?   Supports?   Transitions?

    Were at least five forms of support used?   Explanation?   Description?   Anecdote?
        Instances?   Quotations?   Statistics?   Visual aids?

Conclusion 1 2 3 4 5

    Was the conclusion appropriate?

    Did it round off the speech?

    Did it ramble?

    Was it too abrupt?

Delivery

Appearance 1 2 3 4 5

    Dress; posture

Bodily communication 1 2 3 4 5

    Change of position on platform; basic position of hands; gestures

Vocal communication 1 2 3 4 5

    Audibility; distinctness; pronunciation; meaningfulness

Language 1 2 3 4 5

    Meaningfulness; simplicity and precision; concreteness; figurative language; fluency

General impression 1 2 3 4 5

    Directness; animation; friendliness; sincerity; poise; preparedness

appendix

ANSWERS TO ATTITUDES TEST, PAGE 5

The first two statements are true. The remaining thirteen statements are false.

ANSWERS TO VOCABULARY TEST, PAGES 65–66

1. cogent c: convincing; compelling; forceful; as, a *cogent* argument. Latin *cogere*, "to compel."
2. amelioration c: an improvement; bettering; as, the *amelioration* of international relations. Latin *ad*, "to," and *meliorare*, "to make better."
3. ferment d: agitation; excitement; as, a nation in *ferment*. Latin *fermentum*, "that which boils up."
4. ambient c: moving around; surrounding; encompassing; as, soft, *ambient* moonlight. Latin *ambiens*, from *ambire*, "to go around."
5. cursory d: rapid and superficial; without attention to details; as, a *cursory* examination. Latin *cursor*, "runner."
6. recapitulate b: to sum up; review briefly; as, to *recapitulate* the main points of a speech. Latin *recapitulare*.
7. polemical a: controversial; disputatious; as, a *polemical* editorial. Greek *polemikos*, "warlike."
8. conjecture d: a judgment based on incomplete evidence; surmise; guess; as, a mistaken *conjecture*. Latin *conjectura*, "a divination."
9. sophistry d: tricky argumentation; subtly fallacious reasoning; as, to be adept at evasion and *sophistry*. Latin *sophista*, degenerated in meaning from the Greek *sophos*, "wise."
10. circumlocution c: a roundabout way of talking; use of more or longer words than necessary; as, a wary statement shrouded in *circumlocution*. Latin *circumlocutio*, from *circum*, "around," and *loqui*, "to speak."
11. refute b: to disprove; prove false; as, to *refute* a statement. Latin *refutare*, "to disprove."
12. promulgation a: an official proclamation, as of laws; as, the *promulgation* of a new constitution. Latin *promulgatus*, "made publicly known."
13. anomalous c: deviating from the common rule; abnormal; as, an *anomalous* situation. Greek *anōmalos*, "irregular."
14. espouse b: to advocate, as a cause; as, to *espouse* a new religion. Latin *sponsare*, "to marry."
15. *quid pro quo* d: one thing in return for another, usually of like value; equivalent; as, to receive a *quid pro quo*. Latin, "something for something."
16. capricious d: fickle; whimsical; changeable; as, *capricious* taste in art. Latin *caper*, "goat."
17. redoubtable c: formidable; inspiring respect, fear or dread; as, a *redoubtable* pitcher. Old French from *redouter*, "to fear."
18. equivocate b: to say one thing and mean another; to use ambiguous language with intent to deceive; as, to *equivocate* on controversial questions. Latin *aequivocare*, "to call by the same name."
19. probity d: strict honesty; integrity; as, to have faith in a person's *probity*. Latin *probitas*, "honesty."
20. arrogate c: to take or claim presumptuously; as, to *arrogate* dictatorial power. Latin *arrogatus*, "taken for oneself."
21. *sine qua non* a: something indispensable; a necessary condition; as, "The *sine qua non* of understanding a country is a knowledge of its language." Latin, "without which not."
22. portentous a: ominous; threatening; as, a *portentous* sign. Latin *portendere*, "to foretell, impend."
23. malign c: to slander; defame; criticize maliciously; as, to *malign* the umpire. Latin *malignus*, "wicked."
24. mendicant d: beggar; as, "A former boxer, he is now a *mendicant*." Latin *mendicare*, "to beg."
25. encomium d: formal expression of high praise; eulogy; as, deserving of an *encomium*. Greek *enkōmion*, "laudatory ode."

26. exigent b: urgent; pressing; critical; requiring immediate attention; as, this *exigent* moment of history. Latin *exigere*, "to require."

27. vociferous c: making a loud outcry; clamorous; as, *vociferous* fans. Latin *vociferatio*, "loud shouting."

28. desultory a: without method or aim; fitful; as, a *desultory* pace. Latin *desultorius* from *desilire*, "to leap about."

29. quixotic d: idealistic but unpractical; visionary; as, a *quixotic* plan. From Don Quixote, hero of the Spanish romance of that title by Cervantes.

30. verbiage a: wordiness; unnecessary use of words; as, "His thought was lost in *verbiage*." Latin *verbum*, "word."

31. euphony c: pleasing or harmonious sounds; as, the *euphony* of his phrases. Greek *euphōnia*, from *eu*, "good," and *phōnē*, "sound."

32. elusive b: baffling; tending to slip away or escape; hard to grasp; as, an *elusive* problem. Latin *eludere*, "to evade or escape."

33. subvert c: to undermine; cause ruin; corrupt; as, to *subvert* another's faith or allegiance. Latin *sub*, "under," and *vertere*, "to turn."

34. quintessence c: the purest and best part, as of a substance or quality; the true essence; as, the *quintessence* of delight. Latin *quinta essentia*, "fifth essence."

35. retrospection a: a survey of past events; looking back on old days; as, to indulge in *retrospection*. Latin *retrospecere*, "to look back."

36. animus c: hatred; hostile feeling or intent; as, a violent *animus* in one's heart. Latin *animus*, "spirit."

37. devolve c: to be handed down or delivered over; as, "The decision will *devolve* upon the electorate." Latin *devolvere*, from *de*, "down," and *volvere*, "to roll."

38. vicissitude b: change of fortune; variation in circumstances; as, the *vicissitudes* of life. Latin *vicissitudo*, "in turn."

39. honorarium b: an honorary fee for professional services for which there is no fixed price; reward for gratuitous services. Latin *honorarius*, "honorary."

40. dolorous d: sad; mournful; as, a *dolorous* smile. Latin *dolor*, "sorrow."

41. imputed b: ascribed or attributed (to); charged (usually referring to a fault or misdeed); as, "The crime was *imputed* to him." Latin *imputare*.

42. illusive d: deceptive and misleading; unreal; as, *illusive* hopes for peace. Latin *illudere*, "to mock."

43. nascent d: just starting to develop; coming into existence; as, the early days of our *nascent* Western cities. Latin *nascens*, from *nasci*, "to be born."

44. immure c: to enclose, as within walls; hence, to shut up; imprison; as, to *immure* rioting convicts. Latin *in*, "in," and *murus*, "wall."

45. fortuitous b: chance; occurring unexpectedly, or by accident; as, "A *fortuitous* sixth-inning run eventually won the game." Latin *fortuitus*.

46. invidious b: malicious; likely to cause ill will or to offend; as, *invidious* remarks. Latin *invidiosus*, "envious."

47. cortege b: a procession; (also, a train of attendants; retinue); as, a funeral *cortege*. French, from Italian *corteggio*, from *corte*, "court."

48. ennui d: boredom; feeling of weariness and dissatisfaction; as, to suffer from *ennui*. Directly from the French, *ennui*.

49. canard b: a false story; as, "The newspaper report was a gross *canard*." French *canard*, "hoax" (literally, "duck").

50. insidious d: cunning; intended to entrap; as, an *insidious* argument. Latin *insidiosus*, "artful."

51. salient c: outstanding; important and striking; as, *salient* facts. Latin *saliens*, "leaping forth."

52. aphorism d: maxim; brief, pithy statement of a truth; as, a speech filled with *aphorisms*. Greek *aphorismos*, "definition."

53. efficacious a: producing the desired result or effect; as, an *efficacious* remedy. Latin *efficere*, "to effect."

54. exorcise d: to drive out or expel; as, to *exorcise* the dread of failure. Greek *exorkizein*, "to conjure out."

55. controvert b: to attempt to disprove; dispute; as, to *controvert* an argument. Latin *controversus*, "turned against."

56. digress d: to stray from the main theme of a discourse; as, to *digress* for a moment. Latin *digredi*, from *di-*, "aside," and *gradi*, "to go."

57. spectral b: ghostly; ghostlike; as, a *spectral* gloom. Latin *spectrum*, "image."

58. captious a: unreasonably fault-finding; hypercritical; as a *captious* critic. Latin *captiosus*, "deceitful."

59. averse b: reluctant, unwilling; as, "He was *averse* to taking part in the proceedings." Latin *avertere*, "to turn away from."

60. saturnine d: gloomy; grave; as, a *saturnine* look. From the planet Saturn, considered of melancholy influence in ancient astrology.

1. precise
2. wisdom
3. hector
4. restraint
5. refute
6. sarcasm
7. concede
8. confess
9. endure
10. risky
11. courage
12. humbug
13. passive
14. pastoral
15. devastated
16. perplex
17. oust
18. modify
19. event
20. outlook
21. provoke
22. earned
23. block
24. delusion
25. convictions
26. startled
27. bulk
28. proud
29. notorious
30. blunder
31. ingredients
32. perfidious
33. congregates
34. arduous
35. meddlesome
36. implants
37. link
38. retain
39. requires
40. vindicate
41. ambiguous
42. conciliate
43. meditate
44. impulsive
45. condition
46. discipline
47. apology
48. championing

In evaluating your score two criteria may be helpful:

a. Since there are 4 alternative choices for each item, if you choose answers in some completely random fashion, the statistical probability is that you would get 12 (25%) correct answers.

b. In a pretest on a group of students the median score was 26 correct choices, so that may be considered average. Any score substantially higher then 26 may be considered as good; 45 or more deserves congratulations.

```
    3
B   4
C   5
D   6
E   7
F   8
G   9
H   0
I   1
J   2
```